THE
TREE OF COMMONWEALTH

THE TREE
OF
COMMONWEALTH

A TREATISE
WRITTEN BY EDMUND DUDLEY

Edited, with an introduction

by

D. M. BRODIE
Ph. D. (Camb.), F. R. Hist. S.
*Sometime Research Fellow of
Newnham College*

CAMBRIDGE
AT THE UNIVERSITY PRESS
1948

CAMBRIDGE
UNIVERSITY PRESS

University Printing House, Cambridge CB2 8BS, United Kingdom

Cambridge University Press is part of the University of Cambridge.

It furthers the University's mission by disseminating knowledge in the pursuit of education, learning and research at the highest international levels of excellence.

www.cambridge.org
Information on this title: www.cambridge.org/9781107452695

© Cambridge University Press 1948

First published 1948
First paperback edition 2014

A catalogue record for this publication is available from the British Library

ISBN 978-1-107-45269-5 Paperback

CONTENTS

PREFACE

This edition of *The Tree of Commonwealth* is offered especially
to those who wish to understand the political ideas current
among ordinary men of the late fifteenth century rather than
to those anxious for a philosopher's guidance in interpreting
the constitution of that age. Edmund Dudley, whose career
began in the Inns of Court and ended in the king's service,
was certainly fitted to express many of the conflicting ideals
of his contemporaries. He was a student of the law and
twice lecturer at Gray's Inn at a time when a remarkable
group of Readers, of whom the most notable was Frowyk,
were lecturing during vacations in an endeavour to elucidate
the principles and rationalise the usages of legal procedure.
To do this they called in the assistance of "common reason"
more frequently than older generations of Readers had-done
and defended both age-established customs and the newer
forms of action by appeals to the needs of the "Common
weal" or "wealth". The "commonwealth" envisaged by
these Readers seems to be "society" rather than "state" and
it is in this sense that Edmund Dudley uses the word both
in his French Reading on Quo Warranto and in the title of
his English treatise. Perhaps it was because there was so
little recognition of any serious conflict of interest between
"government" and "governed" that these Readers could
express both their conviction of the greatness of the law and
their willingness to exalt the king's powers and prerogatives,
an attitude also found in *The Tree of Commonwealth*.

It is impossible to acknowledge adequately all the help and
kindness I have received over many years. I owe much to
the valuable advice and criticism which I received from
Mr C. J. B. Gaskoin, the late Mr R. H. Brodie, the late
Dr H. Hall, Dr K. Pickthorn and Professor Putnam. To the
last I owe a special obligation, for she directed my attention
to Dudley's *Law Readings* and constantly helped me from

the stores of her unrivalled knowledge of this type of document. To these, and to many other scholars, I am deeply grateful, but for any errors or misinterpretations I alone must be held responsible.

I must also express my warm thanks to the Hon. Lady Anstruther Gough Calthorpe, to the trustees of the British Museum, to the Librarians of the Chetham Library, Manchester, and of the University Library, Cambridge, and to the Keeper of the Muniments of Westminster Abbey for giving me permission to use manuscripts in their possession or custody. I owe much too, to the kind and efficient help of many officials of these libraries and of the Public Record Office.

Without the very great help which Newnham College has given me, the task of preparing Edmund Dudley's treatises for publication could never have been undertaken. The publishing of this edition of *The Tree of Commonwealth*, put aside when the war brought other duties, is but a recognition of a debt which I can never hope to repay.

D. M. BRODIE

CAMBRIDGE
JUNE 1947

INTRODUCTION

I. Edmund Dudley's Career

EDMUND DUDLEY was born probably about 1462.[1] His father, John Dudley of Atherington in Sussex, was the second son of John, Lord Dudley (de Sutton), a noted Lancastrian noble.[2] His mother, Elizabeth, was one of the daughters and co-heiresses of John Bramshott and through her he eventually inherited the moiety of the manors of Bramshott in Hampshire and of Gatcombe, Calbourne and Whitwell in the Isle of Wight.[3] We know nothing of Edmund Dudley's childhood. His early years may well have been spent in the house at Atherington, to which in later life he brought his first wife, Anne Wyndesore,[4] and it is possible that, like his youngest brother, Peter, he went to Winchester,[5] and then, as Wood asserted, to the University of Oxford in 1476[6] before he began his legal studies. This was a growing practice, and Edmund may have been sent there by his uncle, William Dudley, Bishop of Durham, who in 1483 became Chancellor of that University.

But Dudley could not have remained long at Oxford. At

[1] See Dugdale, *Baronage* (1675), II, p. 217; cf. *Trans. R.H.S.* 4th Series, xv, p. 135, for my first opinion.

[2] See Dugdale, *op. cit.*, and H. S. Grazebrook, *William Salt Society's "Collections"* (1888), IX, pt 2, pp. 65 *et seq.*

[3] For his father's tenancy, cf. Inq. P.M., Chancery II, vol. 22, 12 (10), and Somerset House, Moone, f. 19.

[4] She left a daughter, Elizabeth, who married Lord Stourton. Dudley afterwards married, between 1501 and 1503, Elizabeth Grey, one of the sisters and heirs apparent of John, Viscount Lisle, and had three sons, John, Jerome and Andrew.

[5] See Moone, f. 23, for a bequest to Thomas Emery "for his labour with my son Peers at Winchester". Neither of the Dudleys were resident scholars, see T. F. Kirby, *Annals of Winchester College* (1892), but his brother may have boarded with Emery whose family was well-known in that city.

[6] *Athenae Oxonienses* (1691), I, p. 6.

this period a lawyer's training lasted from sixteen to nineteen years and began in a junior Inn of Chancery where the writs and first principles of the law were studied.[1] About 1478 Edmund Dudley must have entered either Staple or Barnard's Inn, both of which were affiliated to Gray's Inn,[2] in order to have had sufficient experience to be chosen Double Reader by the senior society in Lent 1496.[3]

Dudley had already lectured on Quo Warranto proceedings and this second course of lectures, on the application of the Assize of Novel Disseisin to incorporeal hereditaments, probably helped to establish his reputation as an acute lawyer. In November 1496 he was chosen one of the Under-Sheriffs of London.[4] His election to that important post was the more remarkable because, according to the *Great Chronicle of London*, he was a poor man, "In such caas that he and alle the Frendys he myght make had as mowch to do as they cowde to bryng him Into ye offyce."[5] He was evidently popular with the citizens at that time, for, when he and his colleague, Thomas Marowe, retired in December 1502, they were granted pensions and liveries in recognition of the faithful discharge of their duties.[6]

The turning-point in Edmund Dudley's career came in 1503. Early in the year he, Marowe and eight others received the king's writ ordering them to take upon themselves the degree and state of serjeants-at-law.[7] Then, on

---

[1] Cf. Fortescue, *De Laudibus Legum Angliae* (Clermont, 1869), c. 49, and C. H. Hopwood, *Middle Temple Records* (1904), p. 5.

[2] See R. J. Fletcher, *Pension Book of Gray's Inn* (1901), I, *passim*.

[3] See U.L.C., MS. Hh. 3. 10, f. 96d, "Explicit reportorium Dudley de grays Inn in quadragesima anno Regni Regis Henrici septimi undecimo." See also Dugdale, *Origines Juridicales* (1666), pp. 271, 309, and Fletcher, *op. cit.* I, pp. xxiii–iv.

[4] 29 Nov., 12 H. VII: see Guildhall Records, Journal 10, f. 81d. This reference was kindly supplied by Dr A. H. Thomas.

[5] P. 348.

[6] See Guildhall Records, Repertories, I, f. 116, 13 Dec., quoted by B. H. Putnam, *Early Treatises on the Practice of the Justices of the Peace* (1924), p. 133, n. 5.

[7] See Chanc., Warrants, II, file 252, 13, names only.

4 October, Dudley paid £46. 13*s*. 4*d*. "for an Excempcion from the serjeantship of the Coyff"[1] and Guy Palmes was later nominated in his place.[2] In January 1504 when the last Parliament of Henry VII's reign met, Dudley was chosen Speaker of the House of Commons,[3] and by October of that year he had become a paid councillor of the king.[4]

The reasons for this apparently sudden entry into the royal service can only be conjectured. Dudley's patron was probably Sir Reginald Bray, a friend of his father and grandfather,[5] and he rose quickly to a position of great authority. It is clear that Dudley became one of the legal council which shared with the king's household officials many important public duties.[6] By 1506 he seems to have been president of this council[7] where his principal colleagues were Lovell, Treasurer of the Household, Empson, Chancellor of the Duchy of Lancaster, Hussey, Master of the Wards, and Lucas, Solicitor-General, while Hobart, Ernley or Wyatt sometimes acted with them.[8]

Dudley's accounts, seventeenth-century copies of which are extant in the Lansdowne papers, MS. 127, and in the

---

[1] See Exch. 101, Bundle 413/2, III, f. 46.

[2] See Chanc., Warrants as above, 24 (55).

[3] See Rolls of Parl. VI, p. 521 and *History of Parliament* (1936), I.

[4] Dudley's accounts begin 9 Sept., see Lansd. MS. 127, f. 1. His pension began 29 Oct., see Exch. 404, file 85, nos. 25, 56, and Pat. Roll, 22 H. VIII, pt. 1, m. 25 (4).

[5] See *William Salt Society's "Collections"*, IX, pt 2, p. 74. For evidence of association between Bray and Edmund Dudley, see S.P. 1, 2, f. 6 d, and Exch. 101, Bundle 413/2, III, f. 43. See also Exch. Warrants, 404, Bundle 85, n. 122, and Lansd. MS. 127, ff. 3, 7, 11 d.

[6] Cf. Polydor Vergil, *Angliae Historia* (1555), Lib. xxvi, p. 613.

[7] See the grants to Chirk and Denbigh, Pat. Roll. 21 H. VII, pt 2, m. 5 (17), 18 (4). The offices of those present are recited, beginning with the Chancellor and Privy Seal. Dudley's name follows those of Daubeney, the Chamberlain, and Lovell, the Treasurer of the Household, and this arrangement suggests that he was president of the king's household council.

[8] The list is based on an analysis of the recognisances cancelled, 1-3 Henry VIII. Wyatt, master of the jewels, is the only one whose legal training cannot be proved. He may have owned Dudley's Law Readings, see U.L.C., MS. Hh. 3. 10, flyleaf: "Wyat moy doyt."

Huntington Library,[1] reveal the uses to which his legal
knowledge was put.[2] He was called upon to draw up the
indentures and recognisances which defined the duties of
officials[3] and the terms of the king's loans to landowners
and merchants. He settled also some outstanding debts[4]
and arrears of payments, and secured the money due for
grants of livery, wardship and licences to remarry,[5] as well
as for the restoration of attainted persons[6] and for the re-
stitution of the temporalities of sees and abbeys.[7] More
important than this was his work of levying the fines im-
posed by the ordinary law courts and by the king's council.
The recognisances, which the king's lawyers drew up to
secure these sums, were enforced by the process of outlawry,
a common-law punishment of felons and debtors which
Henry VII made much more effective by demanding heavy
fines for reversing it.[8] Dudley, taught possibly by Frowyk,
Chief Justice of the Common Pleas from 1502 to 1505,
helped to make this policy even more stringent by securing
the king's undoubted right to the goods and chattels, real
and personal, of all outlaws.[9] To this end county officials
were appointed and controlled through a special department
of the king's household under Edward Belknap as "master

[1] MS. EL. 1518, a description of which by the Librarian was kindly
forwarded to me by the late Dr H. Hall.

[2] Cf. F. C. Dietz, *English Government Finance* (1920), University of
Illinois Studies, IX, 3, pp. 38–47.

[3] Dudley also prepared obligations entered into on the sale of offices
and for collecting "gifts" on appointment.

[4] E.g. a debt owed to Richard III was settled, Nov. 1505, see Lansd.
MS. 127, f. 12 d.

[5] For Dudley's share in this work, see also Belknap's accounts, Exch.
101, Bundle 517/14.

[6] See 19 H. VII, c. 28, for Parliament's authorisation of the reversal
of acts of attainder by letters patent.

[7] For a rise in these rates under Henry VII, see S.P. 1, 1, f. 102 *et seq.*

[8] These payments ranged from 10 mcs. to £100. Cf. F. C. Dietz,
op.cit. p. 42.

[9] Cf. Frowyk, *De Prerogativa Regis*, lect. 16, U.L.C., MS. Hh. 2. 1,
ff. 25–25 d, and Belknap's commission, Pat. Roll, 23 H. VII, pt 3, m.
24 (3).

of the prerogative",[1] and their returns enabled the king's ministers to make the fines more commensurate with the offenders' real wealth.

Dudley shared too in the judicial work of the Council in the Star Chamber[2] and in the Duchy Chamber of Lancaster.[3] At other times Empson and Dudley seem to have acted on their own authority in securing the arrest, detention and punishment of those charged with felony or other offences.[4] In these cases there was room for grave miscarriage of justice, as Dudley confessed, though he could with a clear conscience deny that he had connived at it for his personal advantage.[5]

It was especially unfortunate for Edmund Dudley's later reputation that he was so frequently employed in the prosecution of leading London merchants whose violations of the customs and export regulations were generally revealed by "informers".[6] Londoners had other reasons also to be angry with him. First, he was drawn into the bitter feud between the Merchant Taylors and the City authorities.[7]

[1] See Belknap's accounts, Exch. 101, Bundle 517/14. From 1 July 1508 to 10 Mch. 1509, he took, in money and obligations, over £2910: of this about £770 was paid into Belknap's and Heron's hands and another £788 was spent on wages, etc.

[2] See Lansd. MS. 160, f. 320, for fines levied in the Star Chamber which were taken from Dudley's accounts, and Pat. Roll, 20 H. VII, pt 1, m. 13 (24), and 21 H. VII, pt 2, m. 5 (17), 18 (4) for judgments.

[3] For the constant use of this court in Henry VII's reign, see Entry Books, D.L., 5/3, 4.

[4] See Westminster Abbey, MSS. 9260, 12249, and *Letters and Papers, Henry VIII* (1920), I, 731 (20), for Sunnyff's case; also D.L., 5/4, ff. 93, 101 d.

[5] See Lansd. MS. 127, ff. 46, 48, for Sunnyff's payments. There is no means of checking the confession, S.P. 1, 231, f. 167, as the justice of the peace concerned is not named.

[6] Cf. Lansd. MS. 127 *passim* with P. Vergil, *Angliae Historia*, lib. xxvi, p. 621, and Stow, *Annales*, p. 810.

[7] For this account see C. M. Clode, *Early History of the Merchant Taylors' Company* (1888), II, *passim*; Fry and Sayle, *Charters of the M. Taylors' Company* (1937), pp. 34–44; Lyell and Watney, *Acts of Court of the Mercers' Company* (1936), I, pp. 259–60; *Great Chronicle of London*, pp. 332–3; Lansd. MS. 127, f. 16.

This began in January 1503 when Henry VII granted the gild extended privileges, including powers to accept members of other companies and to use the high-sounding title of "Merchant Taylors". The City's stubborn opposition to this grant delayed its enrolment at the Guildhall until 31 March 1505, and in the autumn of the next year these disputes led to an open clash between the king and his capital. This occurred when the king's nominee for the office of one of the sheriffs was rejected because he was a prominent member of the Merchant Taylors' Company. The king immediately sent Dudley to the City to secure the annulment of the first election and Sir William FitzWilliam's success in that held three weeks later.[1] Londoners never forgave this check. Soon they began to mutter that "whoo soo evyr had the sword born before hym, Dudley was mayer, and what his pleasure was, was doon". They believed, too, that though himself "a Cytyzen and Fre man of the Cyte", one of his followers had said that "he trystid to se the aldyrmen were clokes of Cotton Russet In stede of Clokes of Scarlet".[2]

Besides interfering in the internal disputes of the City of London an entry in the "Acts of Court of the Mercers' Company" for December 1508 suggests that Dudley may also have helped to settle Henry VII's new rates for poundage. These had been revised, first in 1503 and then in 1507, by the king's exercise of his prerogative,[3] and so it is possible that this tax was the "Custome" which Dudley had recently discussed with the representatives of the Mercers. These men reported that they had told the minister that "they nor theire compeny thought not them self sufficient to make an Answare in that mater, In asmuche as it longith to the generaltie of all the realme, withoute there were

[1] FitzWilliam paid £100 before 2 Nov. 1506, "for ye kingis gracious favour for being Sherif this yeare", Lansd. MS. 127, f. 31.

[2] *Great Chronicle of London*, p. 348.

[3] See N. S. B. Gras, *Early English Customs System* (1918), pp. 123–6, 694–706.

therefore a generall assemble" and that he had retorted, equally bluntly, that this reply would not satisfy the king who would stop the shipment of cloth.[1] If this interpretation of events be correct the Mercers must have given way, but Dudley's handling of the matter was not conciliatory.

Just as he drew upon himself the hostility of the London merchants, so Dudley provoked the wrath of the landowners by the energy and ability with which he asserted the king's feudal rights over his tenants-in-chief. With this side of the government's activities he had been brought into contact as early as 1501, when he and others had been sent into Sussex to enquire into concealments of the king's lands and prerogatives,[2] and later he did much to develop this work.

By issuing these general commissions to survey his feudal resources Henry VII was but taking up the work of Richard III,[3] and in spite of the great unpopularity of these inquisitions into titles, and the refusal of Parliament to give them its sanction,[4] the king pursued his course fairly steadily.[5] As the reign continued the number of lawyers and officials among these commissioners increased at the expense of the local gentry, and their authority was extended. The commission issued to the eight men sent into Wiltshire in 1508, on which Edmund Dudley, John Ernley, the Attorney-General, and three other lawyers were appointed, is typical of the later ones. These men had power to enquire into concealments by the king's tenants of all lands held of him, all suppressions of rights of wardship and other feudal dues; into all alienations, breaches of the forest laws and intrusions on lands or advowsons which belonged to the king; into the estates of lunatics, idiots and of the king's widows who had remarried without his licence; into all crimes, felonies,

[1] See pp. 319-20.
[2] See Pat. Roll, 17 H. VII, pt 1, m. 11 (20)d.
[3] *Ibid.* 2 R. III, pt 3, m. 24d, general commissions in Devon, Cornwall and Norfolk.
[4] See 19 H. VII, c. 32.
[5] Only commissions to enquire into the estates of particular persons were issued between 1486 and 1492, and between 1497 and 1500.

misprisions and escapes of prisoners and convicts; into the estates of outlaws and into concealments by officials or others of customs, subsidies, fines and forfeitures.[1]

Edmund Dudley, who was so bitterly attacked in the first Parliament of Henry VIII's reign for his share in the work of controlling these commissioners[2] and recording the king's titles in the Chancery,[3] was among those to suffer from the inquisitors' zeal. Indeed the history of his manors of Bramshott, Gatcombe, Calbourne and Whitwell is a justification of the king's policy. Until 1431, when the last national census of the king's tenants-in-chief was held,[4] these manors were clearly understood to be held of the king. However when William Bramshott died in 1451, Bramshott was returned as held of the Wyndesore's manor of Stanwell in Middlesex, and those in the Isle of Wight as held of the Woodvile's castle of Carisbrooke. These verdicts were repeated in 1481, on the death of John Bramshott, from whose daughter Edmund Dudley inherited half the manors in 1501.[5] When, in 1508, there was an active group of commissioners at work in Hampshire, Dudley's title was questioned and he was rightly returned among those who had intruded on their estates without the king's livery.[6] Dudley and his brother-in-law, Sir Andrew Wyndesore, were able to obtain the king's pardon,[7] but the story shows that if even the powerful minister could be called to account, ordinary men might well tremble for their property.

Henry VII's death gave the merchants and landowners their opportunity for revenge. Empson and Dudley were

---

[1] Pat. Roll, 24 H. VII, pt 3, m. 17 (4) d.

[2] See especially 1 H. VIII, cc. 8, 12.

[3] See Common Law Pleadings in Chancery, Bundle I, nos. 30, 32, for Dudley's search into previous records. For the cases of Lord Clifford and Maurice Berkeley, *ibid.* nos. 4, 46, and 5, 10, 29, 35, and also Lansd. MS. 127 f. 22 d., for settlement of the first.

[4] See Maxwell-Lyte, intro., *Calendar of Feudal Aids* (1899).

[5] See V. C. H., *Hampshire*, II, p. 492; v, pp. 246–8.

[6] See Inq. P.M., Chanc., Series II, vol. 22, 12 (10), 3 Nov.

[7] See Pat. Roll, 24 H. VII, pt 1, m. 3 (33), 1 Nov.

arrested and examined before the Council on charges of extortion, which were finally abandoned for one of constructive treason.[1] It was arranged that Edmund Dudley should stand his trial at the Guildhall in London before a special commission on an accusation of having sent messages to about nine knights and gentlemen on 22 April asking their armed support for an attempt to seize the king and his council and to govern according to his will. An indictment was found against him on 12 July and his trial began on Monday, 16 July 1509, when he pleaded "not guilty". On Wednesday judgment was passed against him, though, considering the numbers and position of those said to be drawn into the conspiracy, the charge seems baseless.[2]

After this trial he and Empson, who had been convicted at Northampton, were imprisoned in the Tower of London, where Dudley wrote his notable book, *The Tree of Commonwealth*.[3] Possibly those in court who wished to save them[4] hoped that the storms would blow over, but with the new year a fresh attack began, this time in Parliament. The introduction of a bill of attainder drove Dudley in despair to plan an escape from the Tower. Then, when this manœuvre had failed,[5] Empson's and Dudley's enemies carried their campaign against them into the country during Henry VIII's progress there. The king at last signed the warrant for the execution of his father's ministers, and the sentence was carried out on Tower Hill on 17 August 1510, and Dudley's body afterwards buried in Blackfriars' churchyard.[6]

---

[1] See Herbert, *Henry VIII* (1649), pp. 5–14.
[2] See Baga de Secretis, Pouch IV, 54.
[3] For Stow's judgment, see *Annales* (1592), p. 815.
[4] *Ibid.* p. 812, for rumours of the Queen's interest.
[5] See S.P. 1, 2, f. 7, where Dudley says he afterwards learnt that the attainder passed "but onely the comen house".
For the bill, see Lords' Journals, I, pp. 7–8! Officially the only attainder recited is the conviction at the Guildhall, see Inq. P.M., Chanc. and Exch., and Statutes, 3 H. VIII, c. 19.
[6] See *Great Chronicle of London*, pp. 365–6, and Stow, *op. cit.* pp. 812–15. Herbert, *op. cit.* p. 14, dates the execution 18 Aug.

So perished two distinguished public servants. There were certainly reasons, political and personal, for their unpopularity. Neither merchant nor landowner could be expected to appreciate the strong government which Henry VII had built up at their expense,[1] and Dudley certainly increased the number of his enemies by the methods which he used to build up the great fortune that left him with lands in thirteen counties[2] and goods valued at more than £5000.[3] Much of his wealth may have come from trading ventures,[4] and his will shows that his colleagues had lent him large sums of money.[5] Unfortunately he used his opportunities to buy up the estates of those who had to sell them for the price of a pardon,[6] or to repay a loan or mortgage which the king had made.[7]

On the other hand, there were more attractive sides to his personality. Edmund Dudley enjoyed, but he did not exaggerate, the magnificence of court life,[8] and his will shows him an affectionate husband and father.[9] His loyalty to his master, and the courage with which he defended his

[1] Of nineteen people whose recognisances Dudley had drawn, three had theirs annulled because they had been made without just cause, two "for certain causes and considerations", one after a petition for grace and another because the reason for the bonds no longer existed. The rest paid in full.

[2] Rutland, Wilts., Dorset, Hants., Lincs., Cambs., Oxfordshire, Sussex, Norf., Suff., Surrey, Lancs., and Cheshire. See Inq. P.M., Chanc. and Exch., II, and S.P. I, 2, ff. 5–8.

[3] See Baga de Secretis, Pouch IV, 54, and Exch., K.R., 2/17.

[4] Cf. Lansd. MS. 127, ff. 29, 35 d, 53, Exch., K.R., 2/17, and Letters and Papers, Henry VIII (1920), I, 381 (47).

[5] Ibid. 514 (82), for the King's loan of £1000. See S.P. I, 2, ff. 6–6d, for the following debts: Bray, £260, Sir David Owen, £100, Richard Hyll, £36, Edward Lewkenor, £20, and for lands bought jointly with Sir Robert Southwell.

[6] Lands of Roger Lewkenor, Lord Dacre of the South and Sir Adrian Fortescue are mentioned in his will. For these men's difficulties, see Lansd. MS. 127, f. 54d, S.P. I, I, f. 71, and Exch. 101, Bundle 517/14.

[7] Cf. Lansd. MS. 127, f. 47, and Pat. Roll, 2 H. VIII, pt 1, m. 6, for the Earl of Kent's forced sale.

[8] See Exch. K.R., 2/17.

[9] See S.P. I, 2, ff. 5–8.

servants and friends to the last, were of high quality,[1] while
even his enemies acknowledged the spell of his eloquence.
Nor was his work quite in vain. His methods helped to
give the government financial stability and the power to
enforce order and to encourage trade and industry. By
Dudley's death England lost an experienced and cautious
statesman, whose influence might have had a moderating
effect on the policy of Henry VIII's council.

II. The Tree of Commonwealth

There are extant four manuscript copies of Edmund Dudley's
The Tree of Commonwealth, three of which are closely allied.
This group is represented by the edition privately printed
in Manchester in 1859, the text of which was taken from the
copy now in the Chetham Library, MS. 11376, which the
"Brethren of the Rosy Cross" deposited there. This manuscript is written in a neat, clear hand of the sixteenth century,
probably by a professional scribe. The book, which is
slightly frayed at the beginning, was made of good paper
of the usual foolscap size, and the copyist had to leave certain
blank spaces for words that he could not read, or which
were already missing in the text before him.[2] Of the same
period and character is also the fragment now bound in
Volume 25 of the Yelverton Papers,[3] but, though the scribe
was probably working on the same text as the Chetham one,
he wrote so carelessly and unintelligently that, perhaps for
this reason, the copy was never completed.[4] Then for a time

[1] *Ibid.* f. 7.
[2] See *The Tree of Commonwealth* (1859), pp. xv–xviii. The vellum cover
is now missing, but the book has been carefully repaired and bound.
[3] Ff. 51–75. The MS. has been described by: (*a*) Bernard, *Cat. Libr.
MSS* (1697), II, p. 131; (*b*) Hist. MSS. Comm., 2nd Report, 1871. It is
now at Elvetham Hall, Hartley Wintney, Hampshire, and permission
to see it was kindly given me by the Hon. Lady Anstruther Gough
Calthorpe.
[4] The MS. ends abruptly at the close of a page, *infra*, p. 86, and the
leaves following are left blank.

The Tree of Commonwealth suffered neglect, until, near the middle of the seventeenth century, the third manuscript of this group, now in Volume 2204 of the Harleian collection, was made for Sir Simonds D'Ewes.[1]

The obscurity of the early history of these three texts makes it impossible to determine exactly the relations between them. The Harleian may have been derived from the Chetham version, with which it was certainly collated, perhaps by that William Walker who, in 1627, owned the earlier copy.[2] Yet the discovery of a manuscript, contemporary with that of the Chetham, but independent of it, suggests that behind the formation of this group lay a fourth text, housed in an accessible library. It is possible that the parent copy was once in the Cotton collection,[3] and that it was the one which Stow made in 1562 to present to Robert Dudley, Earl of Leicester.[4]

The fourth manuscript copy of *The Tree of Commonwealth*, on which the present edition of the text is based, now lies in the British Museum, Additional MS. 32091.[5] It was made by William Honnyng[6] whose career was perhaps typical of his times. The son of Roger Honnyng, who had lands in

---

[1] See A. Kippis, *Biographia Britannica* (1793), v, p. 425. The writing greatly resembles that of D'Ewes's secretary, cf. Harl. MS. 164: the marginal notes may be in D'Ewes's hand.
The MS. was bound up in its present volume, ff. 1–88 d, on 24 Mch. 1723/4.

[2] Cf. *Tree* (1859), p. xviii. Evidence for the collation comes from the seventeenth-century marginal headings copied into the Chetham, and from the adoption of words from the Harleian to fill blank spaces, e.g. pp. 37, 40, 73, *infra*, while the footnotes show how often these two give identical renderings.

[3] See Wood, *Athenae Oxonienses* (1691), i, p. 7. All trace of this MS. has since disappeared; see Bliss's edition, 1813.

[4] See *Annales* (1592), p. 815.

[5] Ff. 44–82. It was purchased in 1883 from Sir Alexander Malet, see note to volume and Hist. MSS. Comm., 7th Report 1879, p. 429. It is a foolscap paper volume bound in parchment, on which are scribbled accounts and rhymes now illegible. The water-mark is a mailed fist.

[6] The late Mr R. H. Brodie, then Assistant-Keeper of the Records, first identified the writing.

Alderkirk, Lincolnshire, he was already a yeoman fisher of the Accatery in Henry VII's reign, and rose in the next to be head, or serjeant, of this purveyancing department of the royal household. He also contracted for supplies for the Navy and became fairly wealthy, being assessed at £1000 for the subsidy of 1535. He left the king's service towards the end of 1537 to engage in private trade in France, a move that was possibly unfortunate, for he had, in 1538, to take a post as secretary to Bonner while he was the English ambassador there. After Bonner left he served the Duke of Norfolk in a similar capacity, and possibly these men and Wriothesley, whose service he entered in 1542, helped him to secure the reversion of the next vacancy among the Clerks of the Signet, in October 1541.[1] Then, on 23 April 1543, he was sworn as one of the Clerks of the Privy Council, and held that responsible post until he was disgraced in the early part of 1550. In March 1551 he received fresh grants from John Dudley, Duke of Northumberland,[2] and it is possible that Honnyng's copy was made about this time as a gift for that powerful minister.

Honnyng probably discovered Edmund Dudley's *The Tree of Commonwealth* among the State Papers, to which he would have had official access, but Stow, who also claimed to have copied the original, did not say where he found it. Perhaps this was wise as he "reserved it to himself",[3] and the author's version was afterwards lost. It may have gone, with other manuscripts which Stow had used, to William Bromley of Bagginton House, Warwickshire,[4] for Bernard, in his *Catalogus Librorum Manuscriptorum Angliae et Hiberniae*, published in 1697, mentioned a copy of this book in the library there.[5] When the collection was dispersed in 1903 it had disappeared, and perhaps this manuscript was among those

---

[1] See *Letters and Papers, Henry VIII, passim.*
[2] See *Acts of the Privy Council* (ed. J. R. Dasent, 1890), I–III, and C.P.R., *Edward VI, passim.*
[3] *Annales*, p. 815.
[4] See *The Times*, 4 Dec. 1933.   [5] Vol. II, p. 102.

lost in the disastrous fire which broke out in Bagginton House on St Thomas's Day 1706.[1]

It is fortunate that, in the absence of an authoritative text of Dudley's treatise, the differences between the two versions are not grave. They lie principally in the style of a few complicated passages where, on the whole, Honnyng gives a rendering more in keeping with Dudley's known directness of speech.[2] Not that this is a trifling matter. Much of the charm of *The Tree of Commonwealth* lies in its vivid, rapid character-sketches, and Honnyng has restored many of these more clearly, among them those of the befurred scholars of ten or twelve years of age at the universities,[3] and of the merchant's pampered son, too delicate to wash his hands before breakfast.[4] Dudley's irony also stands out better in the older version than in the more common one, as, for example, in the passage in which hè disclaims his ability to give the king good advice, "my owne lyf being so wyckyd, as hit is openly knone".[5] In both versions, however, Dudley's political and social views can be studied as typical of their century.

Edmund Dudley was neither an original nor a profound thinker. His book is important in so far as it explains the practical problems facing the government, and throws light on the passions, prejudices and ideals with which it had to reckon. *The Tree of Commonwealth*, inspired perhaps by Nebuchadnezzar's vision of his empire as a tree whose height reached heaven and whose fruit provided meat for all,[6] was planned with a medieval love of allegory, and his conception of the functional character of class divisions was inherited from the doctors and preachers of preceding centuries. In theory he maintained the traditional three-fold

[1] See Dugdale, *Antiquities of Warwickshire* (W. Thomas 1730), I, p. 233.

[2] E.g. Dudley's introduction, *infra*, pp. 21–3.

[3] *Infra*, p. 65.   [4] *Infra*, p. 68.

[5] *Infra*, p. 23; the alternative reads: "myne owne lief hath ben soe wicked and soe openlie knowne".

[6] Daniel iv. 10–12 and *infra*, p. 31.

division of society into commons, lords and clergy, while
he was animated throughout his treatise with the hope that,
through the operation of the root of Concord, every man
would be made "content to do his dewtie in thoffice, rome,
or condicion that he is sett in, And not to maling or disdaine
any other".[1] Yet from the description which Dudley gives
of contemporary conditions, we can see how uneasy the
state of lay society really was. Each group was seeking, by
force or fraud, to further its particular interests. On the one
hand were the nobles, ignorant and arrogant,[2] on the other,
peasants, easily roused to rebellion even by worthless
leaders,[3] while pushing their way into the dignities reserved
for the first,[4] and on to the land belonging to both, was a
rising middle-class of large farmers, graziers and merchants
whose duties it was not easy to define.[5]

The fear of social turmoil lay behind much of Dudley's
emphasis on the responsibilities of kingship, especially for
the impartial administration of justice.[6] Respect for the law,
even towards the close of Henry VII's reign, was not a habit
ingrained in the English character, and the king's personal
interest in the administration of justice had been necessary
to curb great offenders[7] and to strengthen the movement
for reforming the common law itself. Yet Dudley held no
brief for tyranny. If the king was to him, as he was to his
contemporaries, the "supreme judge",[8] Dudley yet made it
quite clear that he could not decide any law suit himself,
but must act through deputies,[9] and follow, where possible,
ancient procedure. Not that this was a complete safeguard
for the liberties of the subject. Indeed *The Tree of Commonwealth* is the first English book to point out that the growing

[1] *Infra*, p. 40.   [2] *Infra*, pp. 44–5.
[3] *Infra*, pp. 87–92.   [4] *Infra*, p. 58.
[5] *Infra*, pp. 46–7.   [6] *Infra*, pp. 34–7.
[7] For the case of George, Baron of Bergavenny, referred to the Council
by the King's Bench, see Lansd. MS. 127, ff. 47 d, 53, 53 d.
[8] Cf. Frowyk, *De Prerogativa Regis*, lect. 1, U.L.C., MS. Ee. 3. 46,
f. 100.
[9] Cf. Fortescue, *De Laudibus Legum Angliae* (Clermont, 1869), c. 8.

power of councillors and officials was likely to become as great a danger to the pure administration of justice as had been the territorial influence of great noblemen.[1]

In speaking of the clergy and of the relations between Church and State, Dudley shows the same dependence on traditional views with a realistic appreciation of existing conditions. To an appeal to the bishops and others to attend to their spiritual duties[2] he added another for their discerning patronage of scholars,[3] contending for this object with all the earnestness of the early English humanists, who were then working to ground the new learning on sound moral character. Other passages in *The Tree of Commonwealth* offer some explanation of Henry VIII's success in imposing his theory of a national church on the consciences of so many of his subjects. Dudley was extremely critical of the worldliness of episcopal and monastic households,[4] and was emphatic in his opposition to the employment of ecclesiastics in secular offices,[5] an anti-clericalism surprising in one of Henry VII's ministers. Already Dudley was prepared for a declaration of the royal supremacy over the Church.[6] He held that the king's responsibility for its governance was given him directly by God,[7] and thus he rejected the high church views of the majority of the medieval schoolmen.

Yet it is unwise to assert that Dudley was "a sycophant"[8] because he noted the very great influence of the king in his own day in all matters which touched the material and moral progress of his people. *The Tree of Commonwealth* must be judged rather as a manual written for the education of a

---

[1] *Infra*, p. 35. For a letter to the justices of the peace in Lincolnshire, see Lansd. MS. 127, f. 34.

[2] *Infra*, pp. 42–4.

[3] *Infra*, pp. 60–4. Dean Colet was a guardian of his second son; see S.P., I, 2, f. 5 and Chancery, Warrants, II, 410.

[4] *Infra*, pp. 64–6. [5] *Infra*, p. 25.

[6] This did not mean that Dudley wished the prince to interfere in purely ecclesiastic matters; *infra*, pp. 25–6.

[7] *Infra*, p. 32.

[8] C. Read, *Bibliography of British History*, 1485–1603 (1933), p. 93.

Prince than as a comprehensive political treatise. Dudley did not often see the necessity for legislative reforms,[1] but he was trying to explain to an inexperienced youth the principles of the daily administration of the State. He believed perhaps rather in men than in measures, but throughout his book he never lost sight of the vigorous, undisciplined community, for the fulfilment of whose needs the prince himself had been created.[2] In its identification of the royal power with the well-being of society *The Tree of Commonwealth* shows that the ground was prepared in the minds of many for the idea of the Divine Right of Kings, and in its insistence on the supremacy of legal traditions the future conflict between Crown and Parliament was foreshadowed.

[1] His attitude to perjury is an exception; *infra*, p. 35.
[2] *Infra*, p. 31.

The
TREE OF COMMONWEALTH

EXPLANATORY NOTE

THE TEXT CHOSEN for this edition of *The Tree of Commonwealth*, that of the British Museum Additional MS. 32091, is referred to in the footnotes as A. In these notes C stands for the Chetham MS. 11376, H for Harleian MS. 2204, and Y for Yelverton MS. 25. In the text of A fresh paragraphs occur on ff. 46, 60d, and 75, and blank spaces at the foot of ff. 49, 52d and 80. These divisions have been used and others added, and the text punctuated afresh.

In transcribing these manuscripts certain rules have been observed. Abbreviation marks have been extended and "ff" at the beginning of a word has been translated by the capital letter. Unless they appeared important, neither the corrections made by the original scribes nor the gaps caused by the fraying of the first six folios of C have been noticed. The spelling of the footnotes, and of the words and headings enclosed in square brackets in the text, represents the reading of the first-mentioned manuscript. Unusual spelling in any of the collated MSS. has been shown, but forms used interchangeably have been ignored. These are: wealth, weal: truth, troth: self, selves: thy, thine: appertain, pertain: where, whereas: although, though: afterward, afterwards: together, togethers: sometime, sometimes: or, ere: moo, more: specially, especially: perchance, percase: y^t, that, et similia: into, in: unto, to: upon, on: nor, ne.

[f. 44] The Tree of Commonwealth—a treatise
written by Edmund Dudley
Minister to King Henry
the VII
whilst he was in Prison, in the
first year of King Henry ye VIII.[1]

[f. 46] This boke, namyd the tree of comon welth, was[2] by
Edmond Dudley, esquier, late counsellour to king Henry the
vii[th], the same Edmunde at the compiling herof being
prisoner in the Tower in the furst yere[3] of the reigne of
king Henry theight. Theffect of this treatise consystith in
thre speciall pointes,[4] that is to say: Furst in[5] the rememberance of god and of the faith of his holy Churche, with the
which thing euery Christyan prince hath nede[6] to begynne,
Secondly[7] of some condicions and demeanours necessarie in
euery prince both for his honour and for the suertie of his
contynewaunce, Thirdly of the tree of common welth,
which tochith people of euery degre, of the condicions and
demeanours[8] which thei should be off.

FORASMUTCHE as euery man is naturally bound not
only most hartely to pray for the prosperous contynewance
of his lyege souuereigne lord and thencrease of the comonwelth of his native countrie, but also to[9] the vttermost of his
power to do all thinges that might furder or sounde to
thencrease and helpe of the same, And bycause I am an

---

[1] Written on the parchment cover at a later date.
[2] H, Y: "was made": C torn, "Tree o…made".
[3] H omits "of the reigne", and C torn, "y…kinge", probably did
the same.   [4] C, Y, H add: "which breeflie followeth".
[5] Omitted in C, Y and H.   [6] C, Y, H: "greate neede".
[7] C, Y, H: "secondarilie".
[8] C, Y, H: "demeanours and condicions".
[9] Omitted in H.

Englisheman borne, who sometyme was a seruant to the king of most famous memorie[1] henry the vii[th], late king of this most noble realme of England,[2] naturall Father to my most redoubtyd[3] souuereigne lord, king henry of y[t] name the viii[th], whom our savior Iesu Christ[4] sawfly guyd with the long contynewaunce of vertue and honor, for he is the Prince that shall revive[5] the comon wealth within this his realme (the which long[6] tyme hath ben in sore decay), And for y[t] I bare my hartie goodwill and love towardes the prosperous estate of my naturall countrie, I entend (god willing) to write a rememberance, (albeit perchaunce both rude and vnlernyd)[7] the which, if men be so pleasyd, may be callid the tree of Comon wealthe. But or the manor of this tree be spoken of, furst I shall briefly toche the[8] re-memberance of god and of the faith of holy churche, with the which thing euery christen king hath most nede to begynne; Secondly[9] a word or twaine [f. 46d] of some condicions or demeanours necessarie in euery Prince[10] aswell for his honour as for his assurance;[11] Lastly I will treate[12] of this tree of common wealth. Not[13] for that I will presume or think hit worthie to be sene or lokyd vpon by my said souuereigne lord, or by any of his honorable councell, or yet by any other noble person of this realme, but by some other person[14] y[t] will loke theron for a light pastime, humbly

---

[1] C, Y, H: "Englisheman and was sometyme a poore servaunte with the king of moste noble memorie".

[2] C, Y add: "(whose Soule Iesu pardon)". [3] Y: "redebed".

[4] C, Y, H invert the phrase on every occasion.

[5] C, Y, H: "(For our Lorde graunting) this is the Prince that shall renewe". [6] C, H: "this longe".

[7] H, Y: "decaie, wherof God helping I most [blind and ign]orant in all manner [of] sciences and [cunning after] the manner of an vnlearned body will write [a rude remem]berance". C is torn where brackets have been inserted in this and following notes.

[8] C, Y, H: "it shalbe somewhat shortlie [tou]ched First of the".

[9] C, Y, H: "secondarilie". [10] Y: "in princes".

[11] C, H add "and sure safetie": Y gives "and safety".

[12] C, H: "and thirdlie then to speake".

[13] C, H: "Nor". [14] C, Y, H: "meane persons".

desyering all the readers or[1] hearers therof not to impute
any article therin to my presumption or temeritie, but to
take[2] in gree and excepte my power mynd and [true][3]
entent, and to deme, interprete and expounde the same as
thei by there discrecions should see cause,[4] for I mene not
by any word therin that I knowe nede of reformacion in
any particular person, but only in myself, the most wretche
of all wretches, or that I have any habilitie or any condicion[5] to counsell or aduertise any lyving creature, my
owne lyf being so wyckyd, as hit is openly knone:[6] But
my full purpose, praier and entent, is that[7] all thinges well
orderyd may so contynew and encrease to the Better. [And][8]
yf any thing be amisse, or out of order, lett euery man
therin examyn[9] his owne consciens and remember the
shortenes of this carefull[10] and transitorie lyfe, and pray for
grace to amend, and lett[11] euery person charitablie help[12] to
reforme wheras nede doth require: for he y^t so doth is[13] a
counsellor and a frynd of[14] all worldly frindes, and full
happie is he y^t hathe, and wisely can kepe, such a frinde and
consyder him.

First, to the most[15] worldly ioye and comfortt of all the
inhabitauntes of this realme of England, I vnderstound that
my said souȇreigne lord, in plain prouff, begynnith his most
noble reigne at the rememberance of god, and hath[16] fullie
determynid hym selfe not only to reforme all suche thinges

---

[1] H: "and".   [2] Y: "take it".   [3] C, Y, H.
[4] C, Y, H: "sounde or expounde the same as they shall by theire
discrecions see cause".
[5] C, Y, H: "am of abilitie in anie condicion".
[6] C, Y, H: "Hath ben soe wicked and soe openlie knowne".
[7] Omitted in C, Y, H.   [8] C, Y, H.
[9] C, Y, H: "order, euery man therein esteeme".
[10] C, Y, H: "casuall".
[11] C, Y, H: "and if that".
[12] C, H: "doe helpe": Y, "doth helpe".
[13] C, Y, H: "for whoe soe doth he is".
[14] C, Y, H: "aboue".   [15] Omitted in Y.
[16] C, Y, H: "[that] he beginneth...with the remembrance of god
hath".

as in tymes past haue ben disorderid[1] and abusyd within
this his realme, But also to his greatest merite to restore his
subiectes from[2] diuers wronges and iniuries, and as an
obedient child[3] and willing the comfortt and relief of the
soule of his father, to see the will of his said father[4] and king
to be truly performid, to his mervelous grete mede and
honour, which seldome hath ben seen within this his realme.
But suer may his grace be, he dealith not so charitably and
honorably for his said father, But y[t] god [f. 47] will cause
his[5] noble issue and successours to do aswell and as louingly
for hym, and by this his doing god will increase his grace
singulerly to sett his affection in his love and honour, as to a
christen prince necessarie it belongith.

And ouer this [he] [shall order][6] hym self with his greate
grace to be that catholike king that shall not only support
and meyntein his churche and the trew faith therof in all
rightes as farr as in[7] hym lyeth: but also to see y[t] suche[8] as
he shall promote and sett[9] in christes churche, speciallie
within this his realme, be both conning and vertuouse, and
speciallie[10] vertuouse, for withowt that conning profitith but
litle to the honor of Christes Churche. And for the more[11]
parte such as are promotyd and sett in the Churche of
Christe, and speciallie in the highe dignitie therof, for any
manour of affection, beit for Bloud, seruice, or any otherwise,[12] withowt thei be therwith[13] vertuous and conning,
hable[14] to rule ther Churche, shall do therin more harme then
good. And perillous hit is, and vtterly to be eschewid, to
promote any man that will Labor therfore, and speciallie

---

[1] C, H: "misordered".   [2] C, Y, H: "of".
[3] C, Y, H: "and ouer that as a childe obedient".
[4] C, Y, H: "entendeth to see the will of his Father".
[5] Omitted in C, Y, H.
[6] C, Y, H. A reads "shalbe orderid".   [7] Omitted in C.
[8] H: "church".   [9] H: "settle".
[10] C, Y, H: "in especiall to be".   [11] Y: "most".
[12] C, H add: "cause": Y, "any other cause".
[13] C, H: "there be withall": Y, "thei be with all".
[14] Y: "and able".

suche as will aduenture the danger of Symonie, mentall or [Simony][1]
actuall,[2] to haue promotion. Thei shall neuer do good in
there Cures, and be but the distroiers of the Churche of
Christe. And hit is no harme to be ware of the promoting
of foolke at the speciall labor or[3] desier of any person, be he
of the Counsell or the[4] kinges seruante, for els ther shalbe
often and many tymes set in Christes Churche full vnhable
men for thonlie profyte[5] or affection of the laborers. And
hit is vnfytting and inconuenient[6] to aduance to promocion
any defamyd[7] persons of ther Bodies, or any man[8] to haue
diuerse promocions with cure, except greate cawse require
it. And when thei are promotyd hit werre a meritorious
deede to send them home to ther cures, and speciallie the
prelattes and such other as haue greate Cures, oneless[9] ther
presens may not be forborne about the kinges person for his
greate honor or for the comon wealth of the realme; els[10]
thei ought to be enforced to kepe home for the discharge of
the kinges conscience and theirs, although their appitite
were to the contrary. This should be a good deede, And more
ouer y[t] none of them [f. 47d] be in any temporall office,[11]
nor executors therof, for therby most comonly is[12] destroied
the Churche and thoffice.

Also it were a graciouse and a noble acte that the Churche
of England were restorid to hur[13] free election after thold
manor, and not to be lettyd therof by meanes of you, oure
souuereigne lord,[14] nor by meanes of any of your subiectes
as farforth as you may help yt, and to foresee that no comfort
be gyven to any person y[t] laborith[15] any suche to the con-

---

[1] H.   [2] "mentall or actuall" omitted in C, Y, H.
[3] H: "and".   [4] Omitted in Y.   [5] Y: "the profitt".
[6] C, Y, H: "not fytting or convenient".
[7] C, Y, H: "speciallie anie defamed (H: "deformed")".
[8] C, Y: "nor noe man".   [9] C, Y, H: "without".
[10] C, H: "this realme or els": Y, "his…".
[11] C, Y, H: "offices".   [12] C, Y, H: "is most commonlie".
[13] C, Y, H: "theire".
[14] C, Y, H: "the meane of you Soueraigne lorde".
[15] C, Y, H: "labour".

trary. For therin shall your hyghnes be apposyd[1] by diuerse waies wherof the Verie trueth shall not appere vnto you: for thei will tell you, your letter[2] shalbe but a curtuouse letter of recommendacion: but consyder you well, your[3] request to any of your subiectes is a straict[4] commandyment.

[Approba-cion of bene-fices][7] Also for the honour of god let your grace refraine[5] your self from thappropriacion[6] of benefices or to vnyte any house of religion to[8] another, for if this do contynew it shall by[9] all likelihood distroie the honor of the Churche of England. Also your progenytors vsyd mutche to write to ther subiectes, spirituall and temporall, to[10] haue the disposicions of ther promocions, which was a great discourage[11] for Clerkes, and, god be thanckyd, ther owne promotions were honorable and sufficient for ther owne chappelaines. And for the good increase of vertue amongist the clergie of your realme yt shalbe a[12] greate furtherance to haue in your rememberance[13]

[Vni-versities][14] to protect and also to comfort your vnyuersities and also the studentes therin, and specially divines, for thei decaie fast, [for][15] thei be nedefull for certein condicions or[16] demeanours to euery noble prince, righte necessarie aswell for his honor as suertie.

My daily praier shalbe during my short lyf for y[t] thing which I doubt not your noble grace will remember a thousand tymes better then I can consyder, and y[t] is, y[t]

[Leagues][17] your grace will truly kepe and obserue all leages and promises to owtward[18] princes and straungers made by you or to your owne subiectes promysyd, and[19] [that] all suche leages and

---

[1] H: "opposed".   [2] C, Y: "Lettres".   [3] H: "that your".
[4] C: "streight": Y, "straigt".   [5] Y: "abstayne".
[6] H: "approbacion".   [7] H.   [8] Y: "in".
[9] H: "in".   [10] C, Y, H: "for to".
[11] H: "discouragement".   [12] C, Y, H: "also a".
[13] H: "to haue...rememberance" omitted.
[14] This and the next two marginal headings in C have been entered later.
[15] C, Y, H.   [16] H: "and".   [17] H, C.
[18] Omitted in Y.
[19] In Y, blank space left for "promysyd and".

promyses be don by[1] good advise and deliberacion; And
when thei are made, fyrmely to hold them though thei
should be to your losse, for [of][2] all worldly[3] losses, and
specially in a prince, honor and credence is the most. And,
in the reuerence of god, somwhat beware of daungerous
sportes for casualties y^t mighte fall, and the rather for y^t [Sportes][4]
[f. 48] in your only person dependith[5] the whole welth and
honor of this your[6] realme. And suer I am your grace will
vse, as euer you haue vsid, to lett as few ydle wordes, and
speciallie of slaunder and of vntroth,[7] to passe your mowthe,
as you may, nor to gyve your eares nor[8] your eyes[9] ouer
often to fantasies in the which standith but Vanitie,[10] nor to
be lighte of credence.

And ye of your greate wisedome in all wheightie[11] cawses
take counsell of good and wise men, for[12] thei y^t drede not
god syldome gyve good counsell, and syldome it profiteth
a prince to gyve confydence to young counsell,[13] for experience is one of[14] the chief parties[15] of counsell. Let[16] neuer
christen prince folow the counsell of cruell men nor[17]
couetouse men, for the cruell counsell euer prouokyth[18] the
ire of god [and] The couetouse counsell shall lose[19] the hartes
of the subiectes. The cruell counsell[20] shall instructe there
souuereigne y^t his suertie restith in crueltie, and such counsell
was gyven[21] to king Sawle in the begynnyng of his reigne,

[1] Y: "promises and leages to be made by": C, H "to be made
by".   [2] C, Y, H. H: "for of" repeated.
[3] Y: "your worldly".   [4] C.
[5] Omitted in Y.   [6] Omitted in H.
[7] "and of vntroth" omitted in C, Y: H repeats "of slander".
[8] H: "or".   [9] C: "eyne".
[10] C: "vanities".   [11] C: "welthie".
[12] C, Y, H: "to be councelled of...men and alwaie [H: also] to
followe the counsell of good men for".
[13] H: "and...young counsell" omitted.
[14] Y: "for".   [15] C, Y, H: "partes".
[16] C, Y, H: "But let".   [17] C, Y, H: "or".
[18] C, H: "counsellors euer provoke (Y: provokyth)". C, Y, H read
"counsellors" for "counsell" throughout this passage.
[19] H: "ever leese".   [20] C, H add: "will shewe theire soueraigne".
[21] C: "there given": Y: "then geven".

but he, at y^t tyme^1 being the child of god, refusyd vtterly to reuenge his owne quarelles by crueltie becawse he cam [Covetous]^2 into his realme peasiblie. The covetous^3 counsell will shew there souuereigne his suertie standith mutche in plentie of treasure, but both theis counselles are but fallible fantasies, for the profyte of euery christen prince dependith in the grace of god which is won by marcie and liberalytie. The wroth of all mightie god is gyven^4 by crueltie and couetousnes. Therfore hit is most necessarie for a christen king to haue^5 the love and feare^6 of god before his eyes before^7 whom all thinges do reigne, for the devill, the world and the flesshe will contynuallie fighte and make Battell ayenst all mankynd, and peraduenture more faruentlie ayenst a prince then a pore man. The devill also will bring the prince of this world to his owne propertie yf he can, which is to follow rigor and crueltie, for so doth he, withowt mercie or pittie. The world will enduce them to follow his propertie, which is to sett all there felicitie in worldly treasure, and therin to be insaciable and not to^8 force of the meanes how it shalbe had. The Fleshe, if [f. 48 d] he may by any meanes, wold make princes to follow hur^9 Beastly appetite, for that is the beast of all beastes if hur^9 frailtie be followid.

But for a memoriall to eschew thees thre perillous enemyes let euery king^{10} and prince looke one thend of them that haue ben ouercome and vanquisheid by theis thre ennemyes, or by any^{11} of them. [And] let the kinges of this realme seke no furder, but resort to ther owne progenitours or predicessors, kinges of the same. For the furst, who was more rygorous and cruell then Harrald, sometyme king of this realme? Verily none.^{12} What was his conclusion? A short

---

^{1} C: "being at that tyme". ^{2} H.
^{3} Omitted in H. ^{4} C, Y, H: "gotten".
^{5} C, Y, H: "And therefore...necessarie that a christen kinge haue".
^{6} C, Y, H: "the feare". ^{7} C, Y, H: "by".
^{8} Omitted in C, Y, H. ^{9} C, Y, H: "his".
^{10} C, Y, H: "christen kinge".
^{11} C, H: "or any": Y: "or one".
^{12} Y: "neuer none".

reigne and a cruell. Also the late king Richerd the third followid hym in condicion, and therfore his reigne and end was after the same. For the second, what prince of this realme, or any other[1] realme, was more unworthy[2] then king Henry the third? Neuer any.[3] He was so insaciable y^t he lost therby the[4] hartes of his subiectes, insomutche y^t all his realme reiosyd his deth. Peraduenture of that appetite haue[5] ther ben some other of late tyme, and wer[6] in maner withowt faulte, saving only y^t; But how suche a king shalhaue[7] the louing hartes of his subiectes late experiens may plainly shew hit. For the third, who lesse regardid the loue of god in vsing the frailtie of his[8] Fleasshe then king Richerd the second, which was goodly in personage[9] and right wise and eloquent? For the which he died not only[10] withowt issue of his body to succede after hym, but [by] what inordynate warre and trouble hath[11] ben within this realme sithens[12] his deth for the succession therof the matter apperith and shewith the course[13] of his flesshe. Hit is thought he was both cruell and couetous, and by his end hyt should so appere, for he had a mervelous cruell death. And when he was in his prospirite[14] his subiectes, in comparison both noblest and other,[15] vtterly forsolke hym, and sufferid an other having no title to subdew hym. Also is it[16] not like y^t the ponyshement that the late king of noble memorie, king Edward the fowerth, had in ye fair florishing [f. 49] issue of his bodie, his sones I do meane, motche for loving his[17] fleasshely appetite?

---

[1] Omitted in C, H.
[2] C: "worthe": H: "worth" erased but nothing substituted: Y: "worthy".
[3] C, Y, H: "none".
[4] C, Y, H: "all the".
[5] C, Y, H: "hath".
[6] C, H: "was".
[7] H: "should have".
[8] C, H: "the".
[9] C, Y, H: "person".
[10] C, Y: "all only".
[11] C, Y: "haue".
[12] C, Y, H: "since".
[13] C, Y, H: "cause".
[14] C, Y, H: "highe prosperitie".
[15] C, Y, H: "nobles and others".
[16] C, Y, H: "it is".
[17] C, Y, H: "of his".

Wherfore our lord Iesu save and kepe all Christen princes, and specially[1] our most dreed and naturall souuereigne lord, from theis thre greate ennymyes, and to fixe and stable hym in other thre noble vertues, contrary to these thre condicions. And y[t] in stede of rygor and crueltie he may be pituous and marcifull, And in steade[2] of inordynate desier to these worldly goodes he may be liberall and plentuous, And in stede[3] of thappetite of fleashely[4] desier he may be clere[5] to his owne spouse and quene, which is the furst order of chastitie. What then shall his reward and conclusion be for theis at the Last? For keping[6] his bodie cleane and chast to his wif and quene god shall send hym plentie of faier issue which shall succede hym in honor and vertew, and ouer y[t], shall crowne hym in heaven with the holy king and confessor,[7] S[t] Edward. And for that he wilbe content with his owne trew righte, and not to wrong and oppresse[8] his subiectes, but be to them marciable, liberall [and][9] plentuous, as reason shall require, god will reward hym not only with sufficient[10] plentie of worldlie riches but also with the louing hartes of his subiectes, and thei to serue and obey hym truely,[11] with louing dread, which is the perfytt and suer bond of all gaines;[12] And ouer y[t], god shall crowne hym with Charles the greate king, which was faithfull, iust and liberall in all his actes and lyving. And for y[t] he is mercifull and piteous[13] god him self will ponysshe his enemyes, perchaunce[14] sorer then he hym self would, or at the least will induce[15] them to be his true subiectes and seruantes; and ouer

---

[1] C, Y, H: "moste specially".

[2] C, H: "the steede": omitted in Y.

[3] C, H: "the steede".   [4] H: "the fleshly".

[5] C, Y, H: "cleane".

[6] C, Y, H: "shalbe his conclusion and rewarde, Theise at the leaste for keepinge". H omits "and rewarde".

[7] C, H: "holy and blessed confessour". C: "blessed" written in later.

[8] C, H: "owne right and not wronge or oppresse".

[9] C, H.   [10] C: "sufficientlie".   [11] Omitted in C, Y, H.

[12] C, Y, H: "profit (Y corrected to "perfect") and sure bonde of obedience".

[13] C, H: "plentuous".   [14] Omitted in Y.   [15] C, Y, H: "reduce".

y^t, [he] shalbe crownid in heaven^1 with the holie king and prophet, David, to whom god said: I haue found a man after myne owne harte. INUENI HOMINEM SECUNDUM COR MEUM.

[f. 49 d] And nowe to speke of the tree of comon welth. Hit is y^t thing for the which all trew englisshe men haue greate nede to pray to god y^t our lord and king will haue^3 a singuler regard and favour theron, for princypally by god and hym hit^4 most be holpen. Therefore^5 god hath ordenyd hym to be our^6 king, and therto is euery king bounden, for y^t is his charge, for, as^7 the subiectes are bounden to ther Prince, so be all kinges bounden to ther subiectes by the comaundyment of god them to maynteigne and supporte as farre as in hym is his power. His welth and prosperite standith in the welth of his trew subiectes, for though the people be subiectes to the king yet are thei the people of god,^{8} and god hath ordeyned ther prince to protecte them and thei to obey ther prince. The comon wealth of this realme or of the subiectes or Inhabitauntes therof may be resemblid to a faier and mighte tree growing in a faier feild or pasture, vnder the couerte or shade wherof all beastes, both fatt and leane,^{10} are protectyd and comfortyd from heate and cold as the tyme requireth. In like maner all^{11} the subiectes of that realme wher this tree of comon welth doth sewerly growe are^{12} ther by holpen and relyved from the highest

^{1} C, Y, H: "servauntes over that shall crowne him (Y: in heaven)".
^{2} H, C. ^{3} C, Y, H: "theron haue".
^{4} H: "that". ^{5} C, Y, H: "And therfore".
^{6} Y: "the". ^{7} H: "that as".
^{8} C, Y, H: "are bounde to their Prince of their allegiaunce, to loue dreade serue and obey him or else to be punished by him, as straightlie is the Prince bounde to god to maintaine and supporte, as farre as in him is or lieth, the common wealth of his subiectes. And all they abide and see the punishment of god, for though the people be Subiectes to theire king yet they be the people of god".
^{9} H, C, Y.
^{10} C, Y, H: "a great mightie tree...the shadowe or (H: and) Coverte whereof all the beastes both the fatte and the leane".
^{11} C, Y, H: "Even so all". ^{12} C, Y, H: "be".

degre to the lowest. But for a troth this tree will neuer[1] long
stand or growe uprighte in this realme, or in any other,
withowt diuerse strong rootes, and fastened sewer[2] in the
grounde.

Radix rei-
publicae
amor dei[4]

The principall and cheif roote of this tree in euery Christen
realme[3] must be the love of god, and the love of god is
nothing els but to know hym[5] and gladly to obserue his
[lawes][6] and comaundymentes as his trew and faithfull
people. Ye will saie percase the Bisshopps and thei of the
spiritualite [f. 50] haue speciall[7] charge of this [roote][8] and

[The charge
of which is
in ye king][9]

not the prince. Yes, veryly, the prince is the ground owt of
the which this roote must cheifly growe, for hit is he yt[10]
doth appoint and make the bisshopps, and if the prince in[11]
theis romes ordene vertuous men this roote will kepe, and
if he ordene therto viciouse men or negligent persons[12] hit
will wether and decay. And thoughe the Bishopps wold be
necglygent and not ponnisshe the missedooers in ther dioces,
yet let the prince warne them therof. And if ther be any
sturdie or obstynate persons in his realme yt will frowardly
disobey ther ordenaries[13] in the cawse of god, the prince
must put to his mightie hand to thelpe and reformacion[14]
therof. Whom then doth yt prince assist?[15] The Bisshopps,
curates or preachers? Forsoth none of them. He assistith
his maker and redeamer of whome he hath all his power and
auctorite. And such as be[16] knowne for open synners within

   [1] C, Y, H: "not".
   [2] Y: "rootes fastened": C, H: "sure fastened".
   [3] Y: "chiefest roote...comon Realme".
   [4] H, C: "Roots. The first root is [love and obedience of God]".
The words inside the brackets have been added later in C. Y: "Rootes.
The 1st Roote".
   [5] H: "God".   [6] C, Y.
   [7] Y: "spirituall".   [8] C, Y, H. A reads "tree".
   [9] H. In C "The charge" is written in faintly.
   [10] C, H: "that it is he that".
   [11] H: "if he in".   [12] C, Y, H: "bodies".
   [13] C, H: "ordinarie".
   [14] C, Y, H: "to helpe to the reformacion".
   [15] C, H: "And if there be whome doth that prince then assiste?"
   [16] C: "bene": H: "have been".

this realme, as open murderers, adulterers, Blassephemers, extorcioners and oppressers of his subiectes, let not the prince be famylier [with]¹ them, nor shew vnto them his louing countenance: but let them be rather by them self a lone that men² may know the cawse whie, and yᵗ shall cause them [not]³ onely to amend, percase mutche⁴ rather then all the monysshecions of ther curates or ordynaries, and⁵ also it shall cawse others to beware of like offences, to the grete merite of the prince. Then the roote of the loue [of]⁶ god, which is to know hym with good workes, within this realme⁷ must cheifly⁸ growe by our souereigne lord the king. And for⁹ the sewer and parfitt fastening of this roote in the king one thinge¹⁰ is very necessarie, And yᵗ is, yᵗ [f. 50d] all his subiectes, spirituall and temporall, may see in ther prince yᵗ he hym self settith his principall delight and affection in the loue¹¹ of god, keping his lawes and commandementes. How motche shall yᵗ enforce and encoradge the Bisshopps and other of the spiritualtie to be the verie Launternes of Lighte and to shew good examples to¹³ the temporaltie, and thei to folloo the same. And how motche shame and¹⁴ rebuke should hit be to all those yᵗ wold vse the contrary. And then is this principall roote, the love of god, so sewerly fastened, in so noble and parfytt ground rootyd, yᵗ, with the grace of god, he shall do his deavour¹⁵ to bare vp this tree of comon wealth in this realme of england euer.¹⁶

Besydes this principall roote, this tree suerly to be borne vp must haue other fower rootes, yᵗ is to saie, iustice, trothe,

[good example in yᵉ King]¹²

---

¹ C, Y, H.   ² C, Y, H: "some man".
³ C, H: "not cause them": Y: "not only cause to".
⁴ Omitted in C, Y, H.   ⁵ C, Y, H: "but".
⁶ C, Y, H: "lawe of".   ⁷ H: "within this realme" omitted.
⁸ C, Y, H: "highlie".
⁹ C, Y, H: "lord and out of him. Yet for".
¹⁰ C, Y: "one thing" omitted.   ¹¹ C, Y, H: "lawe".
¹² H, and, in later hand, C.   ¹³ H: "in".
¹⁴ C, Y, H: "or".
¹⁵ C: "devour": H, Y: "endeavour".
¹⁶ C, Y, H: "foreuer".

concord and peace. Furst ye[1] must haue the roote of
Iustitia[2] Iustice withowt the which the[3] tree of comon welth can[4]
not contynew. And this roote of iustice must nedes come of
our souereigne lord hym self,[5] for the whole auctoritie
therof is gyven to hym by god, to mynister by hym self
or by his deputies to[6] his subiectes. And though it be
sufferid[7] or permyttyd y[t] a prince make or ordeyne his
deputies[8] in euery parte of this[9] realme to mynister iustice,
as his Chauncellour, his iustices of both benches,[10] and other
generall and speciall comyssioners in euery [countie][11] and
Shere, yet the cheif charge is his owne. Wherfore, for the
honor of god, lett it be foresene y[t] his grace may make his
Iustices of them y[t] be well lernyd men and specially of good
consciens, or els thei wilbe corruptyd with meede or affection
so y[t] thei mynister[12] to his subiectes great wronges and
synister iustice vnder the [f. 51] color of iustice, and long
peraduenture or it shall[13] be known to the Prince. Also[14]
ther wold be a straight charge gyven to the chancellour
tappoint in euery contrie and sheere wisemen, and specially
good men and suche as will deale indefferently bytwene
the subiectes, and in no wise[15] to put in auctoritie[16] those
which are greate bearers of matters. And when the iudges
resort vnto the kinges grace lett hym gyve them a great
[as did Q. charge to mynister iustice treuly and indifferently vpon pain
Elizabeth][17] of his highe and great displeasure, besydes the[18] danger of

¹ C, Y, H: "he".
² H, C, Y: "four other roots". C adds "justice" in a later hand.
³ C, Y, H: "this".   ⁴ C, Y, H: "may".
⁵ C, H: "lordes self".
⁶ C, H: "or his deputie by": Y: "or his deputy to".
⁷ "suffered" omitted in H.
⁸ C, Y, H: "maie make and ordaine his deputie".
⁹ C, Y: "his".   ¹⁰ C, Y, H: "the benches".
¹¹ C, Y, H. In A: "countrie".
¹² C, Y, H: "Iustices to be well learned men, and of good conscience
speciallie, for else...affeccion, that they shall mynister".
¹³ C, Y, H: "should".   ¹⁴ C, Y, H: "And also".
¹⁵ C, Y, H: "anie wise not...".   ¹⁶ C, H: "any aucthoritie".
¹⁷ H. In C this and the next five headings have been added later.
¹⁸ C, Y: "theire".

y^{er} consciens. Yet by hym the [y]¹ most be enformid and put in corage so to do, and y^t thei lett [not]² for fere or³ displeasure of any of his one seruantes or counsellours to do trew iustice nor for fere of any great persons⁴ in his realme, for y^t that⁵ thei do is don by his auctorite, and not by ther owne. And though the cawse toche⁶ hym self, yet he must put them in comfort not to spare to mynister iustice withowt fere: And this⁷ to do he⁸ shalhave greate meede,⁹ for without doubt fere is a great impedyment of iustice emongist the iudges and commyssyoners.¹⁰ Also of necessite the prince must bare and supporte them in all the mynistring and executing of iustice, aswell ayenst the noblest as other, or¹¹ els it will not be in there poore¹² to do there trew dewties. Also it were a good deede to commaund the privie counsell and [secretarie]¹³ y^t no lettres passe them in stopping of iustice, for by such lettres oftetymes¹⁵ iustice is greatly trobleyd¹⁶ and lettyd, And vnder¹⁷ the color of peticion by specuall labor and affection. Also a singler furtherance to good and¹⁸ indeferent iustice to be had, and to the consciens of the king a greate discharge, shalbe tappoint good Sherifes and such as will not be affectionat or bribers, for in them lyeth mutche to make or marre the conclusion of iustice, [and] that ther be had a speciall [rule] to ponysshe periurie, [for] Persons periurid be²⁰ the vttermost mischeif of all [f. 51 d] good righte and

---

¹ C, Y, H: "And yet therewithall by him they".
² C, Y. ³ C, Y, H: "nor".
⁴ C, Y, H: "person". ⁵ Omitted in C, H.
⁶ C, Y, H: "tocheth". ⁷ C, Y, H: "thus".
⁸ C, H: "they". ⁹ H, Y: "need".
¹⁰ C: "Iustices".
¹¹ C, Y, H: "and aswell (Y: and) against the nobles as other for".
¹² C, H: "powres". ¹³ C, Y, H. In A: "secretly".
¹⁴ H, C. ¹⁵ H: "sometimes".
¹⁶ C, Y: "distrowbled": H: "disturbed".
¹⁷ C, Y, H: "all vnder". ¹⁸ Omitted in C, Y, H.
¹⁹ H, C.
²⁰ C, Y, H: "the conclusion of verie Iustice and that therebe had a speciall rule to punyshe periured persons. Periurie is". ²¹ H, C.

iustice. Yet[1] must the prince ponishe and oppresse[2] all
maynteners and imbracers, and y[t] must be[3] his owne act,
for it is don most comenly by men of great power and
auctorite. Furthermore,[4] besydes all the comen ordering of
iustice to be don and mynysterid within this realme, whether
it be[5] bytwene the king and his subiectes or betwene
subiectes[6] and subiectes,[6] his grace hym self[7] must haue
a singular zeale and regard to protect and defend his subiectes[8] y[t] thei be not oppressyd by greate men and there
superiors. For owt of doubt yf his grace loke not marvelously
well[10] y[er]to, the poore people of his realme shalbe oppressyd
with there lettres, and oftentymes by[11] his seruantes by the[12]
color of his seruice. And specially in this roote of iustice
lett it not be sene y[t] the[13] prince hym self, for any cawse of
his owne, enforce or oppresse any of his subiectes by im-
prisonement or synister vexacion, by privie Seale or lettres
missyves, or otherwise by any of his particuler counsellours,
but to draw them or entreate them by dew order of his
lawes. For thoughe the matter be neuer so trew y[t] thei
be[15] callyd for, though their pain or[16] ponysshement should
be sorer by the[17] dew order of the law, yet will thei murmur
and grudge by cawse thei arre callyd by the waie of extra-
ordynarie[18] [iustice]. Wherfor the most honorable and suer
way for the prince to haue his righte of his subiectes, [or][19]
to ponisshe them for their offences, shalbe by the dew order
and course of his lawes. And lett the subiectes neuer be
lettyd or[20] interruptyd by his writing, tokens, messages, or
commaundymentes to his iudges or other officers, to haue

[King's care
to defend y[e]
poore][9]

[and rule y[em]
by law not
by preroga-
tive][14]

[and never
stop legal
course][21]

---

[1] C, H: "But yet".   [2] H: "suppresse".
[3] C, Y, H: "much be".   [4] C, Y, H: "And furthermore".
[5] C, Y, H: "realme, be it".   [6] C, Y, H use the singular.
[7] Omitted in Y.   [8] C, Y, H: "poore subiectes".
[9] H, C.   [10] Omitted in C, Y, H.
[11] Omitted by C, Y, H.   [12] Omitted by C, Y, H.
[13] C, H: "a".   [14] H, C.
[15] C, Y, H: "are".
[16] C, Y, H: "and though theire paine and".
[17] Omitted in C, Y, H.   [18] C, Y, H: "waie extraordinarie".
[19] C, Y, H.   [20] C, Y, H: "nor".   [21] H.

the straighte course of his lawes, Beit trauerse, tryall, processe, iudgement, sewing of lyuery,[1] or oyerwise. Yet
peraduenture oftetymes the Prince shall haue counsellours
and seruantes y^t in his owne causes will do further then
consciens requirith, and further then hym self wold shold
be don, oftetymes to wynne a speciall thank of[2] the king,
and sometymes for y^{er} proper aduantage and sometymes
for aduenging of ther owne quarelles, groges or malice.
Let [f. 52] theis seruantes or counsellours take hede y^t thei
do the partie no wrong, for the rode[3] of ponyshement
dieth not. Thus the grace of Iusu Christ, the king of heauen,
will help[4] and support the roote of Iustice that[5] being thus
rootyd in hym self shall hold and staie thone quarter of this
tree of comonwelth within this realme.

The second of theis fower rootes is the roote of troth or   Veritas[6]
fydelite, withowt the which roote the tree of the[7] comen
welth in no wise may be susteined or kept uprighte. It is
so necessarie a thing y^t [there is][8] nether realme, Citie,
company, felloship, or particuler person y^t can or may
contynew in honour or honestie withowt hit, insomutche
y^t[9] the paynymes, the Ientiles, the Turkes and the Sarsens[10]
loue trothe, and kepe hit for ther treasure: And yet[11] the
Devill, which is the auctor and father of all fasehed, ys[12]
there master and lord. Then mutche more hought we to
kepe troth, we christen men to whome Iesu Christ is the
Verie master and leader, which is very trothe hym self,[13]

---

[1] C, H: "lawes by trauers, processe, tryalls, Iudgmentes, stayinge of
Lyuerie". Y: "lawes by processe, triall, iugment, suing of liuery...".
[2] H: "from".
[3] C, Y, H: "revenging of their owne grudges or malice, that they
doe the partie wronge Let theise servauntes or Counselours take heede
for the god".
[4] C, Y, H: "And thus...Christ Iesu and the king of the Realme
helpe".   [5] C, Y, H: "the which".
[6] H: "2 roote [is faithfulness]". In C the words within brackets have
been added later. Y: "The 2nd Roote".   [7] Omitted in C.
[8] C, Y, H.   [9] Omitted in C, Y, H.
[10] C, Y, H: "Gentiles, Turkes and Sarrisens".
[11] Omitted in C, Y, H.   [12] C, Y, H: "and".   [13] H: "itself".

[Truth ,what it is][2] from[1] whome very troth procedyth. Troth is none other[3] but a[4] man to be trew and faithfull in all his promisses, couuenantes, and wordes, and the higher in honor the partie is[5] the more is his[6] shame and rebuke to be provid vntrew. Yf ther be no[7] troth what avaylyth interchange of marchandize,[8] what availeth Cities or townes buylt?[9] Yf ther be no trothe what avalith fraternities and[10] felloshipps[11] to be made, and, for the more parte, if ther be no troth what avaleth lawes and[12] ordynances to be made, or to ordeyne parlyamentes or courtes to be kept? If there be no trothe what avalith men to haue seruantes? Yf ther be no troth what availyth a king to haue subiectes? And so, fynallie, wher is no troth can be nether honor nor goodness.

[It must be in ye king especially][13] Where must this roote fasten hym self? Specially in a king and in all his trew subiectes, but cheifly in hym self, for in hym hit is most requysyt for his highe honour and dignitie, and he most be a great occasion[er][14] and helper y^t it must[15] fasten in his subiectes. The Very [f. 52 d] way must be thus,[16] to ponisshe false men and to aduance and promote trew men. That is the best waie, next to the grace of god, to fastene troth in men and men in troth. And who can this[17] do? No earthly man in[18] effect emong vs but our prince and king. And when a king or a prince[19] in his realme do[20] promote false and subtill men and lett trew men slipp,[21] in

---

[1] C, H: "and from".   [2] H; C, in a later hand.
[3] C, H: "other thinge": Y: "no other thing".
[4] H: "for a".   [5] C, Y, H: "is the partie".
[6] C, Y, H: "theire".   [7] C, Y, H: "not".
[8] Y: "interchanges of marchandizes": C, H: "interchaunge of marchandizes".   [9] C, Y, H: "and Townes to be builded".
[10] H: "or".   [11] Y: "fellowshipp".
[12] C, H: "or".   [13] H; C in a later hand.
[14] C, Y, H.
[15] Omitted in C and Y.   [16] C, Y, H: "sure waie must be this".
[17] C: "thus".
[18] C: "none earthlie in": Y: "none earthlie man in": H: "none earthlie thing in".
[19] Y: "prince or a king".   [20] Y: "doth".
[21] C, H: "this realme doth promote false men and subtile and leaveth true men".

that realme or region falshed must encrease[1] and troth decaie, and thus the tree[2] of commen wealth will in no wyse[3] there stand or growe. But now Englishmen, emongist whome this tree of comen wealth is welnie[4] vtterly fayllid[5] and deade, Ye haue a prince and king[6] in whome was neuer spott or bleamysshe of vntroth knowne or found, the which greate vertue and trothe our lord, for his passion, daily in hym encrease with profytt and contynewance[7] therin, and that all the nobles in[8] this realme may folloo hym in ye same, and so euer one to followe and take example of an other[9] from the highest to the lowest subiectes[10] in his[11] realme. Then how glad shall euery noble man be of the company of an other,[12] and one will trust and love an other. What frendship and confydens shall then be[13] betwene men and men[14] from the highest degre to the lowest. How kyndly and how loveingly[15] will murchauntes[16] and craftys-men of the realme by and sell together and exchaunge and bargain one thing for an other.[17] How diligently and busyly will the artificers and husbondmen occupie ther Labor and Busynes, and how well content will men be, from the highest degre to the lowest, to encrease ther howshold seruantes[18] and laborers, wherby all idle[19] people and vaga-boundes shalbe sett a[20] worke. And ouer this, how glad shall all strangers and people of outward nacions be to deale and

---

[1] C, H: "needes encrease".   [2] C, H: "and this tree....".
[3] Y: "case".   [4] C, Y, H: "well nere".
[5] C: "vaded" (?): Y: "valled": H, blank space.
[6] Y: "a king and prince": H: "or".
[7] C, Y, H: "parfit contynuance".   [8] C, Y: "of".
[9] C, H: "euer to follow and take example one of another" (Y: "the other").   [10] C, Y, H: "subiecte".
[11] H: "this".   [12] C, H: "thother".
[13] "H: "shall be then". C, Y: "will then".
[14] C, Y, H: "man and man".
[15] "and how loveingly" omitted in Y: "how" in C.
[16] C, Y, H: "seruauntes".
[17] Y: "bargain ouer the one for the other".
[18] C, Y, H: "householdes in servauntes".
[19] C, Y, H: "our idle".   [20] C: "on".

medle with the comodities of this realme. And so shall this roote of trothe and fedelytie roially[1] and mightely supporte and bare vprighte the second quarter of this noble tree of comen wealth.

[f. 53] The third roote of the fower rootes is the roote of concord or[3] Vnytie. This roote is[4] mutche necessarie to helpe and mayntein[5] this tree of comon wealth, For where discord and division is it wilbe hard and almost impossyble to haue this tree to[6] encrease and contynew. Discord[7] bringith in consyderacion of conspiracye and retencion, which for the more[8] parte engendereth murder, extorcion and ryott, and oftetymes rebellion, of whome for a suertie cometh Idlenes, the verie mother of all vice both in man and whoman, both[10] noble and vnnoble, and the Lyneall [grandam][11] of pouertie and myserie, and the deadly ennymie to this tree of comon welth. This root of concord is none other thing but a good agrement and conformytie emongest the people or the inhibitauntes of a[13] realme, Citie, towne or fellowship, and euery man to be content[14] to do his dewtie in thoffice, rome, or condicion that he is sett in, And not to maling or disdaine any other.

Where must this noble and necessarie roote begyn to sustain hym self[15] or to growe? Forsothe[16] in our souereigne lord most princypall,[17] and then in his[18] subiectes, spirituall and temporall, nobles[19] and other. Thus it[20] must growe and

Concordia[2]

[Idlenes][9]

[Concord, what it is][12]

[1] C, Y, H: "so this roote…shall royallie".
[2] H, C, Y: "3ᵈ roote". H adds "concord" which is copied in a later hand in C.
[3] Y: "and".   [4] Omitted in C, Y.
[5] C, H omit "and maintain": Y: "sustein".
[6] Omitted in C, Y, H.   [7] C, Y, H: "for discord".
[8] Y, H: "most".   [9] H, and C in a later hand.
[10] Omitted in C.
[11] C, H. A: "thraldome"; Y: "gramum".
[12] H, and C in a later hand.
[13] C, H: "the": Y: "of a" omitted.
[14] C, Y, H: "contented".   [15] Omitted in C, Y, H.
[16] C, Y, H: "for a troth".   [17] Y: "principally".
[18] C: "all his".   [19] C, Y, H: "noblest".
[20] C, Y, H: "he".

fasten in our souereigne lord[1] when he seith iustice mynisterid
to his subiectes trewly and indifferently, aswell to the poore
as to the riche, and [doth] favour and cherishe good men
and ponishe the ill,[2] And in cawses toching hym self to
mynister his Iustice discretly medlyd with marcye, or[3] els
his iustice wilbe sore, y^t it will oftetymes appere to be
crueltie rather then iustice. And I suppose ther is no christen
[kinge][4] hath more nede so to do than our prince and
souereigne lord[5], consydering the greate nomber of penall
Lawes and statutes made in his realme for thard and straighte
ponyshement of his subiectes. Also the Prince must specially
see y^{t6} the nobles of his realme be not at variance one with
an other otherwhiles [than] by complaintes to hymself or
suying his lawes, but in any wise suffer not[7] them to reuenge
ther owne quarelles, old or new, by force or [f. 53 d] by
violence; For if men be at ther owne liberties therin beware
the Prince in a while. Also he must see y^t his subiectes be
not oppressid by ther superiors. And if there be any manour
of grudge[8] bytwene his subiectes of the spiritualtie and his
subiectes of the temporaltie for priuilege or liberties yt were
a great help to this noble rote of concord to haue it stablisshed
and reformyd: and no man can do it But the prince, and so
all the Lawde shalbe his[9] and by likelyhod a greate merite to
godwardes.[10] And when his grace seith iustice thus mynisteryd
and sufferith not cruell debates or oppression amongest his
subiectes than is this roote of concord ryollie stablysshed in
hym. And for the comforte of this roote of concord mightely
to beare this tree of comonwelth, the prince hath nede to
see his officers, purueiours and takers to pay his subiectes   [Purveyors][11]
trulie, according to the good ordynance[12] therof made, and

---

[1] Y: "lord and soueraign".
[2] C, Y, H: "evill".   [3] C, Y, H: "for".
[4] C, H. Y: "lord".
[5] Y omits: "hath more...souereigne lord".
[6] Omitted in C, Y, H.   [7] Omitted in Y.
[8] "be not oppressed...grudge" repeated in H.
[9] C, Y, H: "wherfore all the Lawde should be his".
[10] C, H: "towardes god".   [11] H.   [12] C, Y, H: "ordynaunces".

not to vse ther office to the contrarie, and therwith all to kepe his honorable howshold in plentuous maner, and to exhort, se[1] and constraine the nobles of his realme, both [Hospi- spirituall and temporall, to kepe good hospitalitie, and y^t tality][2] shalbe both for hym and hys realme greate[3] honor and sewertie. And yt were tyme it were holpen, for hit is in this realme sore[4] decaid, and shall neuer encrease but by the presydent of the prince and nobles of the realme, and then will euery man after his degree follow the same. But then must seruantes haue competent wages and clothing with trew paymentes[5] of the same, so as thei shall not nede to be theues, bribors, pollers or extorcioners. And for the studie, pain, diligens and labor y^t the prince thus takyth for his subiectes to kepe them in quietnes and suertie thei must, from the highest degre to the lowest, owe vnto hym ther trew fydelitie,[6] allegiance, honour and reuerence, and to be obedient to all his roiall,[7] lawfull commaundymentes and preceptes, and be[8] redie and diligent to the vttermost of ther powers, with bodie and goodes, in the reskew of hym and of his realme, and to yeld and paie to hym truly all rightes,[9] reuenues and casualties, withowt fraude or couen. [f. 54] And thys donne, this roote of concord is well fixed bytwene the prince and his subiectes.

Yet must this roote stretche further as betwene subiectes[10] [Clergie][11] and subiectes,[10] y^t is, all the [Clergie][12] of this realme, in the which ar conteined Archebishopps, bishopps, Abottes, priors, Archedeacons and Deanes, and all priest, relygious and seculers, Who devoutly are bound to[13] pray for the prosperite of our souuereigne lord and for the good helpe[14]

---

[1] Y: "exact, see"; H: "command"; C: "commaunde" (written faintly in a blank space).   [2] H, and C in a later hand.
[3] Omitted in C, Y, H.   [4] H: "sorely".   [5] C, Y, H: "payment".
[6] C, Y, H insert "and": Y also before "honour".
[7] C, Y, H insert "and".   [8] C, H: "to be".
[9] Y inserts "and".   [10] C, Y, H: "subiecte".
[11] H, Y.   [12] C, Y, H. A: "charge".
[13] C, Y, H: "seculars devoutly to...".
[14] C, H: "for good health": Y: "for good help".

and spede of all his subiectes, as well noblest[1] as other,
euery man well to prosper and spede in his[2] lawfull busynes;
And besydes ther praiers to shew them selfes treu[3] priestes
of Christes Churche, aswell in ther owne vertuous lyving as
shewing and preching the word of god truly and plainly to
the temporall subiectes, and boldly and straightly to ponisshe
synne according to ther auctorite and dewtie; and therwith
to kepe all pointes and serymonies belonging to ther pro-
fession, emploieng the[4] profyttes and reuenues of ther
benyfices as thei by ther owne lawe are bound to do: y[t]   Dispositio
is, one parte therof for ther owne lyving in good howshold   bonorum
and hospitalite, the second in deedes of charite and almes to   beneficii
the poore folke, and specially within ther Dioces and cures
wher thei haue ther lyving,[5] and the third parte therof for
the reparacions[6] and building of ther churches and mansyons.
But where is the parte y[t7] thei must kepe[8] for marages of
ther kynesfolke, or to by landes to leave them Inheritars,
or to hepe[9] treasure, peraduenture to a worse purpose? Yf
thei appropre any of[10] ther reuenues or profyttes of ther[11]
spirituall lyvelod to any other[12] purposes I report me to them
self what case thei stand in, which I trust they will eschew.
And when ther apparell and iesture is priestly[13] according
to ther estate, degre and religion that[14] thei be of ther honour
[f. 54 d] or fame is therby[15] nothing apparid:[16] and hit is not
vnfytting y[t] ther were a plain diversitie bytwene ther
seruantes [and the seruantes][17] of other temporall men aswell
in the honestie of ther demeanures[18] as in the sadnes of ther

---

[1] C, Y, H: "nobles".   [2] H: "all his".
[3] C, Y, H: "to be true".
[4] C, Y, H: "and employ their".
[5] C, Y, H: "wher...lyving" omitted.
[6] C, Y: "reparacion".   [7] Omitted in C, H.
[8] C, Y: "kepe or save": H: "kepe to save".
[9] "to hepe" omitted in C, Y, H.   [10] C, Y, H: "parte of".
[11] C, H: "anie theire".   [12] C, Y, H: "of theise".
[13] C, H: "gesture is grave": Y: "precisely".
[14] C, H: "estates and the degree that".
[15] C, H: "therby is".   [16] Y: "impared".
[17] C, Y, H.   [18] C, Y, H: "demeanour".

vestures. And [thus] this[1] roote of concord is fastened righte well in the clergie of this realme.

[Cheualrie][2]   And as to the suer fastening therof in all the Chivalrie of this realme, Wherin be entendyd all Dukes, Erles, Barons, knightes, esquiers and other gentlemen by office or auctorite, thei had nede to lyve in a good conformyte, y^t is to saie, euery man after the honour and degre y^t god and his prince hath callid hym vnto, and after y^t part or porcion to leade his lyef, and not [to][3] maligne or[4] envie his superiors nor disdaign or sett at nought his inferiors. But euery man to know other with his dewtie and to helpe and guyde[5] as his poower may extend; nor entend any murther or[6] mis-chivous deede, nor[7] be oppressors or distroiers of there neighebours or tenantes; nor by any berers or supporters of false quarelles or matters of ill[8] disposyd persons; nor be doers or inducers[9] of periurie ne[10] of falshed, nor be the takers to seruice nor[11] reteynors of facers or of idle loselles, ne partakers of ther subtiltie nor[12] of ther labor. But be gentle and courtuous in Wordes and deedes, both sobre and honest in demeanour and countenance; Be[13] trew and sted-fast in all wordes and promises to the riche and pore, and be the makers of endes and Iouedaies,[14] charitable, bytwene neighbors and neighebors, frindes and frindes; Be the helpers and the relevers of poore tenantes, and also be the manteynors and supporters of all poore folkes in godes[15] causes and matters, And specially of wydowes and orphantes; and also be[16] trew [payers][17] for y^t[18] which thei shall take of ther neighebors and tenantes; And also be the ponyshers of murderers, robbers, and theves, and all[19] other ill disposyd

----

[1] C, Y, H: "thus the".   [2] C, Y.
[3] C.   [4] H: "nor".
[5] C, Y, H: "guide them".   ·   [6] C, H: "no murther nor…".
[7] Y: "or".   [8] C, Y, H: "evill".
[9] C, H: "the doers or thinducers": Y: "the doers or…".
[10] C, Y, H: "or".   [11] C, Y, H: "takers of seruice or…".
[12] C, Y, H: "ne of subtile or".   [13] C, Y, H: "and be".
[14] "and lovedaies" omitted in Y.   [15] C, Y, H: "good".
[16] C, Y: "that they be".   [17] C, Y, H. A: "praers".
[18] Y: "the".   [19] C: "of all".

people,[1] beit thyn owne seruant[2] or other. And then shall thei be mete and able to do ther prince seruice both noblely and honorably in defending[3] the churche and the comynaltie. For be you [f. 55] suer it is not Honorable blood and great possession,[4] or riche apparell, y^t makyth a[5] man honorable, Hym self being of vnhonorable condicions; and the more honorable in blood y^t he is the more[6] noble in condicions ought he to be, and the more shame and dishonour yt is to hym to be the contrary. Therfore,[7] you noble men, for the better contynewaunce of your Blood in honor sett your childeren in youth, and that betyme, to the lerning of vertue[8] and conning, and at the lest bring them vp in honor and vertue. For veryly I feare me, the[9] noble men and gentlemen of England be the worst brought vp for the most[10] parte of any realme of[11] christendom, And therfore the childeren of poore men and meane folke are promotyd to the promocion and auctorite y^t thee childeren of noble Blood should haue yf thei were mete therfore. And thus shall the roote of concord[13] be nobly rootyd in the Chivalrie of this realme.

[Ill education of Noblemen's children][12]

Yet is it[14] requisett y^t this rote also be well rootyd in the commynaltie of this realme, for ther restith the grete nomber. Therin be all the marchauntes, craftesmen,[16] artificers,[17] francklens, graciers, tyllours and other generally the people of this realme. Theis folke may not grudge nor murmure[18] to lyve in labor and pain, and the most parte of there tyme with the swete of ther face. Lett not them presume aboue

[Comonaltie][15]

---

[1] H: "persons".   [2] C, H: "seruantes".
[3] C, Y, H: "both noble and honorable and to defende".
[4] C, Y, H: "possessions".   [5] C, Y, H: "the".
[6] Omitted in H.   [7] C, Y, H: "and therfore".
[8] C, Y, H: "to Learning vertue". [9] H: "I think the...".
[10] C, Y: "more".
[11] C, H: "in".
[12] This and the next two headings added later in C.
[13] C, Y, H: "And thus (Y: then) shall concord".
[14] C, Y, H: "it is".   [15] C.
[16] C, Y, H insert "and".   [17] C, Y, H add "laborers".
[18] C, Y, H: "murmur nor grudge".

ther owne degree, nor any of them pretend[1] or conterfete
the state of his Better, nor lett any of[2] them in anywise
excede in ther apparell or[3] diet, But use[4] them as there
expensis will suerly serue them. Lett theis folke remember
ther rentes and paimentes y[t] thei must make and rather
pinche ther bellies then sell ther necessaries,[5] and lett them
beware of pollers, pillers and of Westminster hall, or els
ther purse wilbe thyn. To sessions and [f. 55 d] sysesse[6] make
thei no hast, except nede[7] enforce them. Let them sequester
them selfes from costly courtes lest care be the caroller[8]
when ther syluer is spent. Let them not cloth[9] them selfes
in Lyuerie of lordes, Better[10] were the lyuerie of ther wyves.
Lett them also beware of vnlawfull games;[11] the tavernes
and ale howses are not to theis folke mutche agrable; yf
thei vse[12] Hawking and Hunting at the[13] lenigth thei may
[saie][14] fie on[15] ther wyninges. And the chief of theis folke,
as the substanciall marchauntes, the welthie grasiers and
farmers, lett them not vse or couett greate lucre of them y[t]
be lesse[16] then thei, but be[17] vnto ther vnderlinges louing and
charitable. Distroie them not with your compt[18] wares and
prises, excessive gyven to a Daie, and to hastely cast them
not[19] in prison for braking of a daie or twoo, [or][20] take no[21]
greate gaine for long daie[22] to be gyven, nor delyuer[23] them

---

[1] C, H: "nor let anie of them presume".

[2] "any of" omitted in C, Y, H.

[3] H: "and".   [4] C, Y, H: "to vse".

[5] C, Y, H: "bellie (Y: bellies) then to sell their necessarie".

[6] C, H: "assizes".   [7] C, Y, H: "that nede".

[8] C, Y, H: "their carroll".   [9] C, Y, H: "cloath not".

[10] C, Y, H: "yet better".

[11] C, Y, H: "And good it were not to vse anie vnlawfull game".

[12] Omitted in Y.   [13] Omitted in C.

[14] C: "will saie"; H: "say"; Y blank for "may say(?)".

[15] Y: "ouer".

[16] C, Y, H: "nor covet ouer great Lucour and be to you vnkinde
that are (Y: be) lesser...".   [17] C: "be they".

[18] C, Y, H: "and destroy them not with your account".

[19] C, Y, H: "excessive from daie to daie given and not ouer hastelie
caste them".   [20] C, Y, H.

[21] C, Y: "a".   [22] H: "time".   [23] C: "or to deliuer": Y, H: "or".

your mony to bare¹ the losse, and you to haue the profytt
and your mony also. Then² beware of vserie, both plain and
cowlerid, for both to god³ be indyfferently knowne. Beware
of disceites of bying and selling, and meng⁴ not your wares
with subtiltie and crafte, with othes⁵ and lies, subtilly for
gain [for]⁶ if your gaines be reasonable, the Better hit will
abyde. Make not your ware to wieght or to false by your
dissemling, [nor] shortly be at a pointe, for yᵗ is but a craft
to poole the poore people with all. And all though your⁷
thrifte generallie increasyth by lending your⁸ wares to
greate men for daies, though your prises you know best
your selfes, yet⁹ secretly to your consciens, [what]¹⁰ a
straping [one] it is. And thoughe you left the purchasing
of landes, and sometymes buyldinges, till¹¹ your riches were
greatly groundyd, it forcyd not mutche. And¹² ye meane
occupiers and bargayners,¹³ make not your bargaines but so
as ye be able to pay, lest Westminster, Sᵗ Katherens or your
boltyd dores be your reckoning place, and then your
credence for euer is gone. Dimynishe¹⁴ not [f. 56] your
stockes for your wyves pleasure, thoughe she behighte you
to loue better then it was erst. All you craftesmen¹⁵ and
artificers, work diligently and treuly. Let not slothe guyde
you nether early nor late; disdaine not to lerne of men yᵗ
haue conning, strangers thoughe thei be; yf your work and
your stuff be substanciall and trew your custymers will not
faile you. Your Bellies and your Backes to your thrifte be
ennymies; Temporance¹⁶ will helpe all. Ye seruing men and

---

¹ Omitted in H; "be" in C, Y.   ² C, Y, H: "and".
³ C, Y, H: "to god both".   ⁴ C, Y, H: "amend".
⁵ Y: "crafty oathes".   ⁶ C, Y, H: "sweetlie forged, for".
⁷ C, Y, H: "ware to rise or to fall by your assemblie shortlie at a
pointe...crafte the poore people to polle, and consider how your".
⁸ C, Y, H: "of".   ⁹ C, Y, H: "but".
¹⁰ C, Y, H: "as".
¹¹ C, Y, H: "buildinge and feasting till".
¹² Omitted in C, H.   ¹³ C, Y, H: "begynners".
¹⁴ C, Y, H: "and mynishe".
¹⁵ C, Y, H: "to love you. All the craftesmen".
¹⁶ C, Y, H: "are enemyes to your thrifte but temporance".

[Servants]¹ seruantes, be trew and diligent to your masters; excede not
your wages in gamyng and exerciseis.² Be not loth to lerne
lest ye be long³ lewd; think ye not your master⁴ to bad lest
ye change for a⁵ worsse. All ye laborers and plowghmen,
delighte in your labors;⁶ be not werie of your swete, yt be
semyth you Best; let not Idlenes lede you in the danger of
indigens. And thus the roote of concord shalbe suerly
groundyd⁷ in the comynaltie of this realme, And this roote
of concord, being principallie fastenid in our souereigne
lord, then⁸ in the clergie, Chivalrie and comynaltie, shalbe
well⁹ able to susteine and bare vp this quarter or parte of
this noble tree of comenwealth.

Pax¹⁰   Yet hath this tree of comenwealth¹¹ greate nede to haue
the fowerth roote, the roote¹² of peax. By this is¹³ vnderstand
good vnytie and peax betwene euery¹⁴ souereigne lord and
his¹⁵ realme and other owt¹⁶ princes and realmes, the which is
a verie necessarie roote for the tree of the comenwealth in
euery region or countrie, for though ther be neuer so good
concord and vnytie amongest them selves, if thei be sore
vexid and troblyd¹⁷ by warres with owtward parties¹⁸ yet
yt wold be¹⁹ a greate impedyment to this tree of comenwealth, and specially in this realme of England, consydering,
lawded by god, yᵗ the comodities of this noble realme are²⁰
so noble and with that [f. 56d] so plentuous yᵗ thei can not
be spent²¹ or all imploied within the same, But necessarily

---

¹ H, C.   ² C, Y, H: "expences".
³ "be long" omitted in Y.   ⁴ C, Y, H: "think your master not".
⁵ C, H: "the".
⁶ C, Y, H: "and ploughmen...labours" omitted.
⁷ C, Y, H: "rooted".   ⁸ C, Y, H: "and then".
⁹ Omitted in H.
¹⁰ H, C: "4ᵗʰ root (of peace)". In C the words in brackets were
added later.   ¹¹ "tree of comenwealth" omitted in C, Y.
¹² C, H: "the root" omitted.   ¹³ Omitted in C, Y, H.
¹⁴ C, H: "our".   ¹⁵ Y: "this".
¹⁶ C, H: "owtward": Y: "other".
¹⁷ C, Y, H: "trowbled and vexed".
¹⁸ C. "partes" throughout this passage   ¹⁹ C, Y, H: "wilbe".
²⁰ C, Y, H: "be".   ²¹ C: "spended".

ther must be entercourse bytwene this realme and outward parties for the vtterance therof, and speciallie for the wull, clothe, tynne, leade,[1] fell and hide, besides other diuerse[2] comodities y^t do[3] greate ease to the subiectes. Howbeit I feare lest[4] y^t the Best comodites of this realme be so motche appayrid by subtiltie and falshod y^t thei be not reputyd, estemyd, or so motche made off as thei Haue Ben. Furst, the woolles of this realme be not so well orderyd in the growers handes as thei haue ben, but for lacke of good order thei be mutche impayred in fynesse, y^t, when yt commyth to thandes of the marchauntes, by them or[5] ther packers yt is subtilly apparyd and alteryd. In likewise the clothes of this realme, what by untrew making and what by the subtile demeanour in thandes of thaduenturers and murchauntes, thei be lytell sett by in all owt parties,[6] not only to the greate preiudize of the king and his subiectes but also to the infamye and rebuke of the people of[7] this realme. I doubt me lesse ther is such craft[8] and subtiltie vsyd[9] in leede and other the[10] comodities of this realme of england.[11] But I pray god yt may be put in the mynd of our souereigne lord to comaund his counsell, with such wise and experte men as thei will call vnto them, to take some pain and studdie[12] for the reformacion herof and y^t bytimes, lest other countries take all the practise of our comodities from vs, And then percase yt wilbe past remedy. And for the[13] reformacion herof the reward of our souuereigne lord shalbe merite, honour and profytt. How greate merite shall yt be to hym[14] to reduce those falsenes to [f. 57] trothes. How mutche shalbe his

---

[1] C, Y, H insert "and" before "clothe" and "Leade".
[2] C, Y, H: "diuers other".   [3] C, Y, H: "doth".
[4] Omitted in C, Y, H.   [5] C, Y, H: "and".
[6] C, H: "outward partes": Y: "owtward parties".
[7] C, H: "of people in...": Y: "of people of...".
[8] C, Y, H: "me ther is like craft".   [9] Y: "subtill vsage".
[10] Omitted in C, Y, H.   [11] C, Y, H: "of england" omitted.
[12] C, Y, H: "studie and paine".   [13] Omitted in C, Y, H.
[14] C, Y, H give the 2nd instead of the 3rd person singular in this passage.

honour y^t by his studie and pollicy the comodities of his realme shalbe in suche good reputacion as thei haue ben in old tyme. What large profyttes and customes by reason herof[1] shall grow to the king by grete entercourse y^t will ensue therby. And after y^t this manour hath[2] ben vsyd the comodities of other realmes arr righte for us, and so to haue entercourse and enterchange thone with thother, which shalbe righte hard to be vsyd and exercysyd profytablely withowte the roote of vttward peax. This owtward peax[3]

[Warre][4] is very necessarie, for warr is a greate[5] consumer of treasure and riches. I suppose righte[6] greate treasure is sonne spent in a sharp warr, therfore lett euery man beware what counsell he gyveth to his souereigne to enter or to begyn warr. Ther are mayny waies to enter[7] into yt, and the begyning semeth a greate pleasure, but the waie is verie narroo to come honorablely owt therof, And then oftetymes full painfull, besydes y^t it is verie dangerous for the soule and bodie. This[8] roote of peace must nedes be rootyd in the person of our prince and by theis[9] meanes, y^t is to say, by such good and suer lyege and[10] amyties and noble alliaunces as his grace by thaduise of his honorable counsell wylhaue[11] with owtward princes. And when thei perceive the wisdome, discrecion, auctorite and courage y^t god hath put in his noble person thei will the[12] more gladly offer hym honorable peax, and not the wursse thoughe in tyme of peax he make good and suer preparacion[13] for warr. And this rote of peax so well radycatyd in his most roioll person,[14] shall well and [f. 57d] sufficiently beare and vphold the iiijth quarter of this profytable tree of comonwealth.

---

[1] C, Y, H: add "and otherwise".
[2] C, Y, H: "Also after this manner that hath".
[3] H: "This outward peax" omitted.   [4] H, C.
[5] C, Y, H: "marvelous greate".   [6] C, Y, H: "a righte".
[7] C, Y, H: "warre, or in anie wise (Y: waies) to enter".
[8] C, Y, H: "the bodie. And this".   [9] C, Y, H: "his".
[10] Omitted in C, Y, H.   [11] C, H: "will make".
[12] H: "then": omitted in Y.   [13] C, Y, H: "preparacions".
[14] Y: "his noble person".

But let us know when this tree hathe his being, [with] theis fyve rootes[2] so suerly staid and fastened within thys realme, what fruete shall growe on the[3] same tree. This tree shall beare fower plentuous frutes corespondent to the fower last rootes, for like as by the moistenes[4] of the roote euery tree Bearith his frute, even so by the vertue of the furst[5] of theis iiij[er] rootes this tree shall beare the fruete of honorable dignitie; by the vertue of the second roote, which is troth, this tree shall stand and bare[6] the fruite of worldly prosperite; by vertue of the third roote, which is concord, this tree shalbring furth the fruite of tranquylite; and by the[7] vertue of the iiij[th],[8] which is peax, this tree shall bring forth the fruite of good example. And notwithstanding [that] theis iiij[er] fruites, thus plentuously growing owt of this tree of comon wealth by the vertue of theis[9] iiij[er] rehersyd rootes, bee asmutche benefycyall[10] and profytable for our souuereigne lord and all his subiectes in soche maner as afterword shalbe rehersyd: Yet, consydering y[t11] he is one of the most Christen kinges, and all his subiectes arr Christen people, of necessytie this tree must bare this fruete[12] of comon wealth the more[13] suerly fixid and rootyd with theis iiij[er] last rootes, and plentuously garnished with theis iiij[er] rehersyd fruetes which was[14] often and many tymes found emong the turkes and Sarasyns, for all those sectes haue motche delyte to vphold the tree of comen wealth. Yet[16] peraduenture some wold saie y[t] ther tree hath not the roote of trouthe in keping of ther promes and behestes.

[The Fruites][1]

Quattuor radicum fructus

[Turkes][15]

---

[1] H, C. The singular is used in Y.
[2] C, Y, H: "tree being with the fowre rootes...".
[3] C, H: "this".
[4] C, Y, H: "for in (H: even) likewise as by moistnes".
[5] C, Y, H: "of the first" omitted.
[6] C, Y, H: "shall soone beare".
[7] Omitted in C, Y, H.   [8] C, Y adds "root".
[9] C, Y, H: "the".   [10] C, Y, H: "bewtifull".
[11] Omitted in C, H.   [12] C, Y, H: "first fruite".
[13] C, Y, H: "the more" omitted.
[14] C, Y, H: "were".   [15] C.
[16] C, Y, H: "amonge the Turkes and yet".

I wold we had yt as suerly.[1] Hathe not ther tree the rote of concord and vnytie emongest them selves? Yes to well, the more pittie it is. Hath not ther tree the roote of outward[2] peace, for the more parte at ther owne[3] willes and pleasures? Doth not ther tree bringforth theis fower fruetes rehersyd?[4] Yes, withowt faile [f. 58] and abundantly. First honorable dignitie; who hath had [it] so excellently?[5] None, as toching bodely honor and dignitie. Ther tree hath worldly [prosperitie][6] and doth bare it aboue other, and hath don of long contynewaunce.[7] Haue not thei in ther tree the fruite[8] of good example? Yes doubtles, after the manour and[9] cerymonies that thei kepe. Then this tree of comon wealth bringith forth theis iiij^{er} fruetes. And yet be thei neuer so[10] plentuouse thei be not necessarie for our catholike [king] and this his[11] Christen realme withowt the furst[12] fruite, which is most delycate and best for a christen prince and his subiectes: which fruete is the honour of god. And this fruete is so[14] plentuous y^t it woll not faile to come and growe in this tree by[15] vertue of the furst roote, which is the love of god, and y^t must be to loue and know hym by faithfull workes and not[16] by glorious wordes and curious cerymonies. This[17] fruite will neuer growe in the tree of comenwealth emongest paynymes and[18] gentiles, Turkes and Sarasyns, and all[19] becawse thei want the roote of the[20] trew loue and[21] knoledge of god, which roote thei or any of them, without it were certene particuler persons callid by grace, could

[Honour of God][13]

---

[1] C, Y, H: "roote of Iustice. Yes verily and peradventure more suerly fastened with them then with us".

[2] Omitted in C, H.   [3] Omitted in C, H.

[4] C, Y, H: "rehersed fruites".   [5] C, Y, H: "excellent men".

[6] C, Y, H. In A: "exsperite".

[7] C, Y, H: "beare abundantlie of longe contynuance".

[8] C, Y, H: "spirit".   [9] C, Y, H: "of their".

[10] Y: "the more".   [11] Omitted in C, Y, H.

[12] C, Y, H: "fiveth".   [13] H, C.

[14] Omitted in C, Y, H.   [15] C, Y, H insert "the".

[16] Omitted in C, Y, H.   [17] C, Y, H: "and this".

[18] C: "or".   [19] C, Y, H: "or Sarrisons all".

[20] Omitted in C, Y, H.   [21] C: "or".

neuer attain vnto. And for a short conclusion, that tree y^t
lackyth this roote shall neuer bare this fruite. But this tree of
comon wealth, hauing this principall roote of trew loue and[1]
knolledge of god by faithfull and charitable workes, and
therby plentuously bring[ing][2] forth the fruite of the honor
of god with thother iiij^{er} rehersyd fruites, is now mete and
verie necessarie to growe in this realme.

But how shall theis v maner of fruites be bestowid
emongest our souereigne lord and his subiectes? Shall
euery man take and[4] pull from this tree at his libertie of
euery of theis fruites and y^t as largely as his self lustith,[5]
hauing no regard to the state or condicion y^t[6] the person is[7]
of? Nay truly, theis fruites must be taken [f. 58 d] discretly
and as often tymes as the personage requireth, or els thei
will do more harme then good. And now to y^t purpose
shall I speke of the iiij^{er} last fruites, and leave the cheif and
principall[8] fruite till afterward.

And as toching[9] the furst of theis fower fruites, which is
honorable dignitie, ther may none[10] of the subiectes, spirituall
or temporall, presume to take one pece of this fruite by his
owne power or auctorite, but must haue it by delyueraunce
of his souereigne terrestre. The[11] hole sort of this fruite is
ordenyd and seruith[12] for hym self and where it pleasyth[13]
hym to dispose it, and thei to whom he lustith to gyve it
may receive[14] it and none other. For of[15] what person in his
realme, being his subiectes,[16] may it be truly said he[17] is
enteryd into any[18] honorable dignitie, spirituall or temporall,
withowt he sett and receive[19] the same of his handes, or of

[The fruites
devided][3]

Honorable
dignite

[1] C, Y, H: "or".   [2] C, Y, H: "bringeth".
[3] C, Y.   [4] C, Y, H: "or".
[5] C, H: "him liste": Y: "he list".
[6] Omitted in C, Y, H.   [7] C, Y, H: "be".
[8] C, Y, H: "principall and chief".   [9] Omitted in C, Y, H.
[10] C, H: "no manner": Y: "no man".
[11] C, Y, H: "souereigne onlie. Therfore the".
[12] C, Y, H: "shewed".   [13] C, H: "please".
[14] C, Y, H: "retain".   [15] C, Y, H: "by".
[16] C, Y, H: "subiecte".   [17] C, H: "said truly that he".
[18] C, H: "an".   [19] C, Y, H: "saith that he receaveth".

thandes of his progenytors? And in y^t that none of his subiectes may presume to take any parte of this fruite but by his delyuerance it[1] followith perfectly y^{t2} the matter of this roote is[3] Iustice. For who of his subiectes may mynyster any point[4] of Iustice bytwene partie and partie except he haue his auctorite from his souereigne? And theis be two of the highest regalties and begyven[5] to hym only from above, wherfore the charge of his grace is the more right well to foresee to whome he delyuerith or comyttith the roote which is the mynistracion of Iustice, or whom he regardith[6] or aduansyth with the fruite which is honorable dignitie.

Worldly prosperite[7]
As to the second fruite, which is worldly prosperite, this fruite seruith[8] most properly for the Chivalrie of this realme, which be Dukes, Erles, barons, knightes and so forth.[9] Thei may take righte plentuously of this fruite withowt delyuerance so y^t one of them vsurp not to take his superiors parte, for it will agre very ill[10] at length therle to take the fruite of the prosperite of a Duke, or [f. 59] the Baron of the Erle, or the knight of ye baron; euery man must be content of[11] the fruite of his owne properte. And this fruite foloith this[12] roote, which is troth, righte ordynatly,[13] For thoughe falshod, who to troth is contrary, doth righte evill with euery person, yet doth it worse[14] with the noble knightes, and the more noble thei[15] be the worse doth falshod beseme them. Wherfore all[16] you of the chyvalrie, kepe you most specially the roote of[17] trothe and ye can not lack the fruite of worldly prosperite, and that in plentuouse manour.

[1] C, H: "then it".   [2] Omitted in C, Y, H.
[3] C, Y, H: "which is".   [4] H: "part".
[5] C, Y, H: "highest of his Regall[it]ies and given".
[6] C, H: "rewardeth".
[7] H, C: "second—worldly prosperity".
[8] C, Y, H: "sheweth".   [9] C, H: "etc."
[10] C, Y, H: "ill agree".
[11] C, Y, H: "man to be contented (Y: content) with".
[12] C, Y, H: "his".   [13] Y: "ordinarily".
[14] C, Y, H: "worst".
[15] C, Y, H. The second instead of the third person used in C, Y, H.
[16] Omitted in C, Y, H.   [17] C, Y, H: "roote of" omitted.

As for the third fruite of this tree, which is suer[1] tran- Tranquilite, though it be a[3] profytable fruite for euery [of][4] the quilite[2]
subiectes, yet it is most necessarie for the greate nomber of
the commynaltie of this realme, For thei be most in nombre
and can least[5] help them selves. And for them it is so necessarie y[t], if thei lack it, farewell the greatist parte of bying
and selling emongest them,[6] Farewell the conning of
Craftesmen,[7] farewell the [tra]vaile[8] of the artificers, farewell the good trew seruice of laborers and seruantes, farewell
the good trew[9] diligence of Tylth and Husbandrie, and, in
effect, farewell all the honestie[10] and trew diligens emongist
the comynaltie. There arr two maner of fruites of tranquylite: the one is tranquilite[11] in ease and pleasure, But of
this fruite I do not meane for y[e] comynaltie to medle therwith[12] but vtterly to refuse it as thei wold veneme or poison.
Also this fruite of this manour of tranquilite growith not in
this tree withowt yt be in a watery boughe not truly rootyd.
But yf any suche happen to growe, gather them not, but
lett them hang styll for Iaies and pies, or for suche of your
wyfes or doughters as do not force for [thrifte].[13] But
thother tranquilite is ment[14] for you, and y[t] is, to haue
tranquilite to applie diligently with trew labors and honest
diligens and busynes.[15] This 4th [f. 59d] rootes[16] fruite is
ordenyd for your foode, and the rather shall ye haue it yf
the roote of concord be[17] fastenid well[18] emongist you in the
forme aboue rehersyd.

[1] Omitted in C, H.   [2] H; C inserts "3ᵈ".
[3] Omitted in H.
[4] Almost invisible in text owing to erasure of blot by knife.
[5] C, Y, H: "best".   [6] H: "men".
[7] C, Y, H: "craftie men".   [8] C, Y, H: "availe".
[9] Omitted in C, Y, H.   [10] C, Y, H: "honest".
[11] Y omits "the...tranquilite".   [12] C, Y, H: "with".
[13] C, Y, H: "which do not force thrifte". A: "thurst".
[14] C, Y, H: "meet".
[15] C, Y, H: "true labour and honest busynes".
[16] C, Y, H: "4 rootes" omitted.
[17] Omitted in Y.
[18] C, H: "well fastened".

As[1] for the iiijerth and last of theis iiijer fruites, which is the fruite of good example, it is the naturall fruite in the which[3] the Clergie should feede. And though some parte therof be reseruid for the Chyvalrie and comynaltie, Yet the greate[4] store and porcion therof shall serue for them, as of right it besemyth; and of this fruite thei may as plentuously as thei list take,[5] and the more thei vse therof, the more good shall yt do them; and this fruite may thei more boldly and largely medle with[6] if thei do their dewtie for the good preseruacion of the roote y[t] yt springith[7] owt of, which is the roote of peace. What is ther[8] dewtie to do for[9] the preseruacion or[10] contynewance of y[t] roote but to shew in them selfes the parfytt tokens of peax, which be paciens, vnytie[11] and reuerence, and besydes y[t], to pray devoutly for parfytt peax.[12]

So theis be the iiijer last fruites of the comen wealth[13] by the vertue of the iiijer last rootes therof, and ye see by what persons thei shalbe taken. But yet all the subiectes must order them selves well with good awaight[14] in gathering[15] or taking theis[16] fower fruites, y[t] is to say, euery man to gather or take[17] y[e] fruites mete for hym self, and with discrecion, and specially to be ware of suche of thother fruites as are not mete or appropriatyd[18] for them, or els thei will infect and not nourrishe.

First, the Clergie to be content with there[19] fruite of good example, and not covet or desier the fruite of honorable dignitie which is all at the discrecion of ther souuereigne.

---

[1] C, H: "and as". [2] Y, H. C inserts "4th".
[3] C: "in which": H: "on which". [4] C, H: "greatest".
[5] C, Y, H: "they maie vse...as them (Y: they) list".
[6] H: "which". [7] C, H: "sprunge": Y: "sprang".
[8] C, H: "the". [9] Y: "which is to do for".
[10] H: "of". [11] C, H: "humylitie".
[12] C, H: "pray duly for the parfitte peace".
[13] C, H: "of this tree of commen welth".
[14] C, H leave blank space: Y: "wayt". [15] C, Y: "the gathering".
[16] C, Y, H: "of theis". [17] H: "take or gather".
[18] C, Y, H: "fruites that be not appropriated or meete".
[19] C: "the".

Yf thei except yt when it is frely offeryd then[1] it is tyme enough, and to rathe, without thei therto be[2] able and mete: and, thoughe thei be neuer so able, let them in no wise desier yt by any waies or meanes, for, yf thei come by hit so, thei incontynently be cast[3] into the danger of Sicknes[4] of [f. 60] Symonie, or els into a great spice therof. May thei take or receave[5] of the fruite of worldly profytt[6] cheifly appropriatyd to the Chyvalrie? Nay Veryly, if thei entend to occupie well ther owne fruite, which is ye fruete of good example, for thei will not gladly agre[7] togethers. Also in them it is a great preparatyve towardes the infyrmyte of incontynency.[8] How shall thei be partakers of[9] the fruite of sure tranquilite most[10] necessarie for the commynaltie? Of y^t fruite thei may be sufferid to take some parte, so yt be to thentent to vse ther owne fruite of good example the more largely, and[11] els not. How be it yet oftetymes tribulacion is to them but a fruite of good example.

As for [the][12] Chivalrie, let them beware how the[y][13] medle with the fruite of honorable dignitie, And[14] though it be otherwhiles tollerable for them to desier yt when thei arre mete therfore, yet is it more lawdable to haue it of the fre disposicion of ther souuereigne: but in all cases lett them not[15] presume to take it of ther owne auctorite for then it will suerly choke them. How shall thei take vpon them to medell with the fruite of good example y^t the clergie doth? Though thei medle therwithall thei shall not spede the worsse. And as for[16] the fruite of suer tranquilite, of his nature he is to worldly honour a kind frind.[17]

---

[1] C, Y, H: "them".
[2] Y: "to rare except they be therto": C, H follow A until "be thereto".   [3] C, Y, H: "thereby be casten".
[4] C, Y, H: "dangerous sicknes".   [5] C, H: "resigne".
[6] C, H: "prosperitie".   [7] C, Y, H: "will hardlie agree".
[8] C, H: "inconstancy".   [9] C, Y, H: "they be with".
[10] Y: "also".   [11] Y: "or".
[12] C, Y, H.   [13] C, Y, H.
[14] C, H: "although".   [15] C, Y, H: "neuer".
[16] Omitted in C, H.   [17] H: "of freind".

As[1] for the comynaltie, ther o[w]n[2] fruite is most kindly
for them. And as for[3] the fruite of honorable dignite, let
them in any wise neuer desier to except it, for, how so euer
thei haue it, thei haue a lable therwith,[4] and yᵗ is, NON[5]
PRODEST or NON DECET. How shall thei order them selfes
for the fruite of worldly prosperitie to[6] Chyvalrie belonging,
which thei mighte desier?[7] Though the honest marchauntes
and suche other [f. 60 d] of greate substance do deale therwith
yet to the multitute of the comens it is nether profitable nor
necessarie, for the fruite of suer tranquilite is sufficient for
them. May not thei vse the fruite of good example yᵗ
growith for the clergie[8] through the [ir][9] trew diligens? with
diligent labor by motche of[10] there good example percase
with faith it sufficith. But let them not smatter in[11] matters
of dyvynite lest thinfection of heresies[12] crepe in with all.

Now haue you how euery man of theis iiijer fruites shall
take or receaue:[13] but how thei shall vse them it is necessarie̅
to know. As it was before rehersyd, Thei must be vsyd with
discrecion, or els thei will norishe but littell, and or it be
spoken how theis iiijer last[14] fruites shalbe vsyd yt is convenient to speake of the furst. The furst and principall fruite
[Honour
of God][16] is[15] the honor of godd, which in order[17] is the furst and most
excellent fruite in comparison, and[18] the other ar but poison
and[19] veneme to be resemblyd to a perfect medicene. For

---

[1] C, Y, H: "and as".   [2] Written "theron".
[3] C, Y, H: "them: for as to...".
[4] C, H: "for how so euer they haue it, a labell therwith"; Y: "for
how cam they euer...".
[5] C, H: "not".   [6] Y: "for"; C: "to the".
[7] C, Y, H: "for they might desire it".
[8] Y: "yᵗ...clergie" omitted.   [9] C, Y, H.
[10] "motche of" blank in C, H. Suggested reading of this sentence:
"[Because] diligent labour be [a great part] of their good example,
percase...".
[11] Y: "any".   [12] Y: "dragges".
[13] C, H: "restraine".   [14] Omitted in C, Y, H.
[15] C, Y, H: "of the first and principall fruite (Y: pointe) that is...".
[16] H, C.   [17] "in order" blank in C, H. Y: "in word".
[18] C, Y, H: "wherefore".   [19] C, H: "or".

this is the very true and¹ comfortable fruite, without the which all the other are nothing to be regardid, but vtterly to be dispisyd; and specially with a cristen king and in a Christen realme. And this fruite for² his holsome nature is next and redie for euery christen³ man yᵗ will take it; aswell for our souereigne lord as for the Clergie; aswell for the chyvalrie as for⁴ the comons; aswell for the nobles as for the vnnobles; aswell for the poore as for the riche; aswell for the yonge as forr the old; and aswell⁵ for the sick as for the whole. A⁶ precious fruite of noble nature yᵗ shyneth⁷ to all manour of men yᵗ will take it. The more a man deliteth⁸ with it the more holsome it is and the more a man eatith of this fruite the more gredie he is in yt: the more gredy the more good it doth hym. The faster he gatherith the more plentie he leavith. This is a delycate fruite for a christen king. This is the fruite yᵗ preseruith all other fruites. This is the fruite yᵗ all men should insaciably desier. This is the fruite yᵗ costith nether⁹ gold or syluer, praier, seruice, ne labor.¹⁰ This is the fruite yᵗ euery [f. 61] man may take withowt delyuerance of other, or without displeasure or preiudicie to any person. This is the fruite yᵗ neuer tornith¹¹ to surfett, corruption, desease or sicknes. This¹² is the fruite that is both mete and drink, and trew medicene both early and late. Wherfore furst seke for this fruite yᵗ is so good, profitable and [easy]¹³ to be founde,¹⁴ and all thother iiijer fruites, with¹⁵ all there necessaries, shall plentuously be addid to you.

¹ Omitted in C, H.   ² C, Y, H: "of".
³ Omitted in C, Y, H.   ⁴ Omitted in C, H.
⁵ C, Y, H omit "and as well".   ⁶ C, H: "Oh".
⁷ H, C, Y: "that is most wholesome (Y: is indewed) and sheweth". In C "most wholesome" has been written in a blank space.
⁸ C, Y, H: "dealeth".
⁹ C, H: "useth neither": Y: "nether useth".
¹⁰ C, Y, H: "nor silver...nor labor".
¹¹ H: "bringeth any". C has the same reading inserted, by a later hand, in a blank space. Y: "causeth".
¹² C, H: "for this".   ¹³ C, Y, H: "scase" in A.
¹⁴ H: "gathered". Inserted later in C.   ¹⁵ C, H: "and".

[The maner to use the 4 fruites][1]   But nowe speake we of the manor of[2] the other iiijer fruites, that ar so perillous and[3] dangerous of ther owne nature that thei may not in any wise be vsyd after the manor of the rehersyd excellent fruite, and y[t] for many causes but specially for twain. Thone is thei arr so delicious that [they][4] must nedes be vsyd with sharp sauce or[5] els thei be[6] Verie poison[7] and nether medicynable nor meete. The other cause Cores is all theis iiijer fruites haue perillous corys within them y[t] may in no wise be tochid but of necessytie be[8] vtterly refusyd, for thei be venemous in the highest degre y[t] no cause will help them. Also[9] it is verie necessarie to pare thies fower last fruites, and yet for all y[t] thei[10] must be vsyd with poynante[11] sauce. But[12] Forasmotche as the iiijer paringes [and][13] the iiijer corys of theis iiijer fruites ar so dyuerse and of seuerall[14] properties or natures, and y[t] one maner [and][15] kind of sawce must and will serue for all fower[16] fruites, [The 4 paringes][17] First I will speke of the iiijer paringes of theis iiijer fruites, and after y[t][18] of the iiijer perillous cores, and after of the necessarie and poynante[11] sawce y[t] will serue for theis fower fruites.

First, as toching the paringes[19] of theis fruites of honorable dignitie, which fruite is most conueniently ordenyd for our souuereigne lord to dispose at his libertie, yf[20] the paring therof be noble, hauing many noble vertues, yet shall it be righte necessarie vnto hym, as he vsyth it, to[21] pare and louse

---

[1] Y, H, C.   [2] C, Y, H: "speake of the manner of the use of".
[3] C, H repeat "so".   [4] C, Y, H.
[5] C, Y, H: "pained sauce for".   [6] H: "are": C omits.
[7] Y: "poysonable".   [8] C, Y, H: "must be".
[9] C, Y, H: "And also".   [10] C, Y, H: "that".
[11] C, Y, H: "pained".   [12] Omitted in C, Y, H.
[13] C, Y, H. A reads "of".
[14] C, Y, H: "of diuerse and seuerall".   [15] C, Y, H: " of".
[16] C, Y, H: "theis fowre".   [17] Y, H, C.
[18] H: "then of": Y: "and that". In C "then" has been written in paler ink above "that" underlined.
[19] C, Y, H: "And first...paring".
[20] C, Y, H: "dispose, then if (Y: of)".
[21] C, Y, H: "for to".

the paring[1] from [the][2] fruite and to dispose and distribute
the paring to other[3] y^t haue nede therof. The paring of this
fruite is compassion or pittie, the which paring right well
besemeth the roiall fruite of honorable [f. 61 d] dignitie.
But[4] it is to be doubtyd y^t this fruite wearith sore, for[5] yf
the paring of pitie and compassion[6] do not growe this
fruite of honorable dignitie would be alteryd in name and
in nature, as from honorable dignitie to cruell[7] tyranie,
which is cleane contrary to the nature herof.[8] This paring
must be paryd and[9] lowsyd from the fruite, for yf it cleave[10]
or stick fast to the fruite yt will do but lytle good or none,
and when it is paryd it must be distributyd to all them y^t
haue nede of it, and not to be casten in a corner and throwne
to the dogges,[11] for it is ordeyned for the childeren of man.[12]
But yf a question be askyd which of the subiectes haue nede
of this paring, I think it is hard for any of them, spirituall or
temporall, from the highest degre to the lowest, if all
thinges come to light clerely to excuse hym, But y^t ones
in the yere he hath nede of parte[13] of thies paringes. And
thei y^t fall into the greatist danger haue most nede therof.
Yet I meane not to gyve it all tymes to all them y^t nedith[14]
it least Iustice wold seasse; notwithstanding[15] it besemith a
christen king rather to gyve to mutche then to lytle. But[16]
let them neuer want it what tyme malice and falshod haue
brought them to the[17] nede therof, for discrecion by a good
mocion may devide theis paringes. But for a suertie thoftener
a[18] prince parith his fruite and the paring[19] by discrecion be

[1] Y: "for to loose the paringes".
[2] C, Y, H.   [3] C, H: "the other".
[4] C, Y, H: "for".   [5] Omitted in C, H. Y: "of".
[6] C, H: "compassion and pittie".
[7] C, Y, H: "But this fruite of honorable dignitie to turn cruell".
[8] H, Y: "therof".   [9] C, H: "or".
[10] H: "be close". C, Y: "close".
[11] C, Y, H: "casten to the doges".   [12] C, Y, H: "men".
[13] "of parte" omitted in C.   [14] C, H: "at all tymes...need".
[15] C, Y, H: "but yet".   [16] C, Y, H: "but yet".
[17] C, Y, H: "hath brought them the".   [18] H: "that a".
[19] C, Y, H: "and then the paringes".

disposyd, the better will his fruite Be, and the more will it haue the sent of his naturall[1] propertie.

[2nd paringe
—good
example][2]
What is the paring of[3] good example to the Clergie appointed?[4] Encrease of vertue and conning. Of it self it is righte lawdable and the paring righte propre for good example. What shall you of the clergie do[5] with theis paringes? Is there any folke y[t][6] haue nede therof? I trow neuer more nede, and so greate nede y[t], if ye devide not your paringes righte hastely, I feere me the grounde did conning[7] will fall in this realme. Loke well vpon your two vnyuersyties, how famouse thei haue ben and in what condicion thei be now. Wheare be your famouse men y[t] were wont to reade dyvinytie in euery cathedrall Churche and in other great monasteries? Where be the good and substanciall scollers of gramer y[t] haue ben kept in this realme before this tyme, not only in euery good towne and Citie and in other places, but also in all[8] Abbeyes, priories [f. 62] and collages, in[9] prelates howses, and often tymes in howses[10] of men of honor of the temporaltie? Wherfore ye[11] greate prelates, with thelpe of other of the clargie, pare of thies paringes of the encrease of vertue and conning and throw them into your vniuersyties in plentuous manour, and[12] so y[t] euery one of you in your dioces do this aswell in your Cathe[d]rall churches as in Abbeis and priories, and in all other places conuenient. Yf[13] you pare your paringes so ye[14] think y[t] ye take some fruite[15] of good example therwith your paring wilbe the more profytable.

Ye y[t] be the great pillers of the Churche[16] will percase

[1] C, H: "materiall".   [2] Y, C.
[3] C, H add "the fruite of".
[4] C, H: "but the". In C inserted later in a blank space.
[5] Omitted in H.   [6] Omitted in C, Y, H.
[7] H: "increase coming": Y: "groundly cunning". In C "increase" inserted later in a blank space.
[8] Omitted in C, Y.   [9] C, Y, H: "and priories, in".
[10] C: "the howses".   [11] C, H: "the".
[12] Omitted in C, H.   [13] C, Y, H: "and if".
[14] C, Y, H: "I".   [15] C, Y, H: "of your fruite".
[16] C, Y, H: "Clergie".

saie vnto me ye would righte fain y^t conning were encreasyd
yf ye wist how to bring it abowte. Two or three waies will
I[1] shew you y^t will not hynder. First and principallie haue
delyte in vertue and connyng your selfes. And thoughe
your conning were righte good, yet by encrease and Studie
ye shall make it the[2] better, for the greater your clergie is
the more conning you behovith, and the more pain should
you[3] take therwith: let y^t be your pastymes and pleasantes
disportes. The second, favour your conning Clerkes and
promote them with promocions, and searche in the vnyuersities and other places suche as be vertuous and conning
not gyven to fleasshelynes. Make them[4] your Archedeacons
and Deanes, and gyve them your prebendaries. Let them
haue cure[5] vnder you of the sick soules: thei know what
medicenes be necessarie. Haue[6] plentie of suche aboute you:
theis[7] galanttes should be your gard from danger to defend
you. And ouer this to[8] exorte all other in your dioces that
haue promocions in[9] likewise to order them selfes. Let[10] not
to departe with some of[11] your syluer to comfortt and relief
poore[12] schollers, and especiall suche as be willing and apt to
lerne which lack[13] exhibicion: lett them haue what[14] is
necessarie. Thus spend you[15] yerely [some][16] parte of your
porcions thoughe you leave purchasing of landes and
[mynishe][17] your Diott: for a better Chauntree shall[18] ye
neuer founde.[19] Thus[20] distribute you the paringes of your

---

[1] C, Y, H: "I will".   [2] Omitted in H, Y.
[3] C, Y: "you shoulde": H: "you shall".
[4] C, Y, H: "with your promocions and churches in...for such as be
vertuous and connynge make them".
[5] C, Y, H: "care".   [6] C, Y, H: "and haue".
[7] C, H: "for theis": Y: "for such".
[8] Omitted in C, Y, H.   [9] Omitted in H, Y.
[10] C, Y, H omit "selfes" and read: "Thirdlie let".
[11] C, H: "part of".   [12] C, H: "your".
[13] C, Y, H: "a spie such...with like".
[14] H, Y: "which": in C "which" has been substituted in margin for
"that".   [15] Omitted in C, H.   [16] C, Y, H. A: "your".
[17] C, Y, H. Y omits "and". A: "mynisheing".
[18] Y: "can".   [19] H: "find".   [20] C, Y, H: "and thus".

fruites, connyng to encrease. And do not this only your self: but also diligently exhorte all other in your dioces, y^t be able, to folloo the [f. 62d] same, and thus distribute you the paringes of your fruites, connyng to encrease.[1] O how mutche shall your owne excesse[2] of Studie and Labor for connyng enforce all other clerkes in your dioces contynually to Labor and Studie[3] for thencrease of there owne connyng. How[4] mutche shall your promotyng of vertuous and connyng clerkes in greate nombre encourage the Studientes of your vnyuersyties to take pain[5] and diligens to encrease in vertue and connyng. How[6] motche shall your large exhibicions gyven to poore schollers and Studientes encourage young folkes tapplie ther lerning and to be vertuous. And then may you the Better be namyd the strong pillers of the clergie of Christes Churche.

But I pray god hartely y^t none of you turne the paringes of the fruite from thencrease of conning to the discrease and distruction of conning and distribute theis paringes aswell vnto the Vniuersyties as to euery place of your dioces. When do ye so? When so euer you of your self that lack connyng will take no pain to haue it, nor will favor nor cherisshe other to haue it.[7] This is one perillous stroke y^t lettyth the encrease of connyng. And other[8] is when ye dispose your benifyces to suche as ar not clerkes, hauing litle conning and less vertue; and[9] to suche as will sett ther hole mynd and become[10] good and profytable Stewardes of howsholdes and clerkes of kichens,[11] and haue well the conning of breifmentes[12] and casting of[13] accomptes; or to suche as with good pollicie can survey your Landes and can well increase

---

[1] C, Y, H: omit "and thus...encrease".
[2] C, Y, H: "exercise". [3] C, H: "to study".
[4] C, Y, H: "and how". [5] Y: "paynes".
[6] C, Y, H: "and how".
[7] H omits "nor...haue it". [8] C, H: "another".
[9] C, Y, H: "But". [10] C, Y, H: "can be".
[11] C, Y, H: "houses and clarkes of your kitchins".
[12] C, Y, H: "abrevement".
[13] H omits "casting of".

your fynes and casualties, and will sett[1] them selfes in your
temporall courtes; and to suche as can suerly and wysely be
your receivor of your rentes and reuenues, and rather then
faile will bodely[2] distrain a poore mans cattell and dryve
them to pound tyll thei starve for hunger. This is a mischevous
Buffett to thencrease of conning. And yet otherwhiles ye
haue so many former promesses to performe and so many[3]
frindes to please, y[t] your cheif promocions go y[t] waie. And
I will not beleue but y[t4] ye promote some of thies riche
drovers y[t] lend you mony towardes your bulles for your
Love.[5] Theis paringes be thei y[t] can not be callyd thencrease
[f. 63] of your conning,[6] nor of vertue, But the distrucion
and discrease of them bothe.

When de ye throwe thies vnhappy paringes into the
vnyuersyties? When ye cawse[7] theis maner of clerkes ther
to be graduate and[8] not by ther lerning, and y[t] thei may were
furres [in their hoodes][9] and be callid masters in lesse then a
yeres lerning. Thus haue thei[10] ther connyng and lerning
bothe. Other whiles[11] ye send to the vnyuersyties yong
schollers of x or xij yeres of age righte nere of your blood,
and thei must be highely[12] promotyd with an Archedeaconie
or prebend before[13] he can saie his mattens. He must go in
his greyned clothes lyned with silke or furrid with the Best
as though he of y[t] vnyuersytie were the Best, Yet his connyng is but small. But[14] if he be fornishid with vertue he is
not farr a mys. How be suche simple paringes distributyd
abrode in your dioces? When suche as can litle are promotyd to the greate course of dignitie and,[15] because he must

---

[1] C, H: "sit".   [2] C, H: "boldly".
[3] C, H: "greate".   [4] Omitted in C, H.
[5] C, Y, H add "for their bondes will breake".
[6] C, Y, H: "to thencrease of coninge".
[7] H: "see".   [8] Omitted in C, Y, H.
[9] C, Y, H.   [10] C, Y, H: "learning they haue".
[11] C, Y, H: "and otherwhiles".   [12] C, Y, H: "highlie be".
[13] C, H: "ere": Y: "or".
[14] C, Y, H: "as (H: omits) though to that vniuersitie his coninge is
(Y: be) but small, yet".
[15] C, Y, H: "great cures (Y: course) and".

attend his seruice, he will sett one vnder hym that can lesse
y^{en} hym self, or els hym¹ y^t will serue for least² wages.

Theis be perillous paringes to throo emongist the poore
people. I trust ther are none suche in this realme y^t gyvith
suche paringes. Yf³ ther be, lett them leave it assone as thei
may,⁴ for, besydes the danger of ther⁵ consciens, yt may
torne them to mutch⁶ infamye, perchanche more then thei
haue deseruid, For oftentymes the poore people will iudge
the likelyhode. Yf ther be such a prelate promotyd for
likelyhod of profytt thei will iudge y^t he hath his dignitie by
paymentes of mony or els for profytable seruice more then
for any conning or vertue: thei will also saie the same by
there prelates if thei Busie them selves so with ther young⁷
kinesfolkes; and lewd persons⁸ will say it (some⁹ of them)
though it be not true. Wherfore, for discharging of your
soules and [f. 63 d] also for keping of your name,¹⁰ pare well
your fruite of good example and distribute your paring,
which is thencrease of connyng and vertue, as is before¹¹
rehersyd.

Trew
defence¹³   What ys the paringes¹² of ye fruite of worldly prosperite
which ye of the noble chivalrie haue? It is trew¹⁴ defence;
not to defend a false quarell nor to defend a murderer, a
thef, or¹⁵ an extorcioner, But to defend the poore¹⁶ people
from all wronges and Iniuries; and otherwhiles in a iust or¹⁷
trew cawse it is sufferable one of you to defend an other, and
euer to be reddy to defend your prince, the churche and the
realme. And thoftener you pare this fruite and diligently

¹ C, Y, H omit "that can...hym".   ² C, Y, H: "lesse".
³ C, Y, H: "devide such paringes and if".
⁴ Y: "can".   ⁵ Y: "the".
⁶ C, Y, H: "such".
⁷ C, Y, H: "if they so promote (C: in different ink: Y: use) their
young".
⁸ C, Y, H: "bodies".   ⁹ C, Y, H: "soone".
¹⁰ C, Y, H: "for discharge of...your good name".
¹¹ C, Y, H: "before is".   ¹² C, Y, H: "paringe".
¹³ H, C: "Third".   ¹⁴ Omitted in Y.
¹⁵ H: "and".   ¹⁶ C, Y, H: "But (Y: to) defend poore".
¹⁷ C, Y, H omit "just or".

dyvide it, the better is the fruite and the more conuenient for you noble [men]¹ to vse.

Asfor the fruite of profytable tranquilite, it³ is necessarie for the⁴ comynaltie to haue a paring right agreable for yᵗ fruite, and requisit for them It is⁵ to pare and distribute it, which is callid trewly exercise. To what persons shall thei distribute theis maner of paringes? To none other but to ther owne childeren and seruantes, for the good lyf of all⁶ the commynaltie in substance standith in trew labor and lawfull busynes,⁷ and it is behovefull for them to exercise the same both erly and late, and⁸ from tyme to tyme, and not to slugg⁹ in there beddes, but to be therat full trewly in the morning; and then most conueniently¹⁰ is there best spede or iorney. Yet this is not the tymely exercise yᵗ I meane to be the paringes of the fruite of profitable tranquilite, but it is to sett your¹¹ childeren which be yong betymes to some trew labor or¹² busynes, and yᵗ as soune as thei haue any¹³ discrecion to do any thing. And let not¹⁴ there men or seruantes¹⁵ savor or delyte in the perillous paring of idlenes, for if thei haue¹⁶ a felicite therin in there youth it is a greate marvell if euer thei fall to be good laborers or artificers, but will rather serue a gentleman, and yᵗ in the worst maner. For¹⁷ a trew conclusion, the more parte of the men¹⁸ childeren grow to be beggers, theves, or bothe, and the women to be brothels, and at the last begg for there bred. Ye were better gyve them to the gallows then to bring them vp in idlenes.

[4ᵗʰ for the comminalty]²

¹ C, H.   ² H, C, Y.
³ C, H: "that".   ⁴ C, Y, H: "your".
⁵ C, Y, H: "it is for them".   ⁶ Omitted in C, Y, H.
⁷ C, H: "labours and Lawfull busynesses".
⁸ Omitted in C, Y, H.   ⁹ H omits "to": Y: "lugg".
¹⁰ C, Y, H: "right early (Y: truly)...for then most contynuallie (Y: conueniently)...".
¹¹ C, H: "their".   ¹² H, Y: "labours and...".
¹³ Omitted in C, H.   ¹⁴ Omitted in H.
¹⁵ C, Y, H omit "or seruantes".
¹⁶ C, Y, H: "once haue".   ¹⁷ C, Y, H: "And for".
¹⁸ C, Y, H: "for the more(H: most) parte of (C: omits) the men...".

And ye honest marchauntes and other wealthie comyners, be not a shamid to gyve your[1] childeren parte of theis paringes; lett not the [femynine][2] petie of your wyves distroie your childeren; pompe[3] not [f. 64] them at home in furrid cotis and ther shertes to be Warmyd agenst ther vprising, and suffer not them[4] to lie in there beddes tyll tenne of the clock and then a Warme brakefast or there[5] handes be Washid. His nature is so tender he may nether lerne nor labor; Master John he must be callid, and his father, Ser marchant. Set[6] ther bodies to some busynes and y^t bytymes. Remember your selfes how you wan your thriftes. Dandle them not to derely lest folie fasten one them. For oftetymes all y^t ye leave, although[7] ye warr long in getting therof with mutche penurie and pain, shortly thei will[8] spend it with vnthriftie maner, [as] experience will shew more then all this.

Ye nobles of the chyvalrie, thoughe[9] the paringes of this be a presydent to you it will do no harme. I[10] assuer you idle[ne]s bredyth vices aswell in gentiles as in asore y^t be tochid.[11] But asfor you, poore comyners, cast the paring of your fruite to your childeren as ye loue there Lyves. If thei will grudge at this diatt, lett good stripes be ther second seruice. Thus I haue[12] don with the paringes of theis fower fruites.

The iiij perillous cores[13] Wherfor now it is tyme to speke of[14] the iiij^{er} perillous cores. And thoughe the supreme[15] fruite of honorable dignitie belonging to kinges and princes be right presious and glorious, and ye paring therof righte lawdable and worthie,

---

[1] C, Y, H: "to your".   [2] C, Y. In A: "femyne".
[3] Y: "pamper".   [4] C, Y, H: "them not".
[5] C, Y, H: "his".
[6] C, Y, H: "fathers servauntes set".
[7] Omitted in Y.   [8] Omitted in C, Y, H.
[9] Blank space in C, H. Y: "thrust".
[10] C, H: "paringes of the president to you it will doe you no harme, for I". Y follows A until "for I".
[11] C, Y, H: "in other somewhat afore that was touched".
[12] C, Y, H: "have we".   [13] Y, C: "4 coores".
[14] C, H: "somewhat of".   [15] C, Y, H: "former".

yet the core is very perillous to be tochid or vsyd.[1] It is namyd vnreasonable [elacion].[2] It is in no wise good to vse it with your fruite of honorable dignitie; yet throw it not away, it may fortune to serue righte well for some other purpose. But commytt it to the custodie of your reason with a greate charge to kepe it suerly till you shalhaue[4] nede therof. And command your reason to lock it fast in the cofer of your rememberance,[5] And for more suertie let hur sett therin[6] hur foote of subiection. For the naturall[7] propertie of this core is to exalte and lyft vp, if he may by any meanes, the fruite of honorable dignitie aboue his naturall place, and not only aboue the same but also aboue his knowlledge,[8] and will not rest so, but, if he haue libertie, he will suerly sett hym aboue the highest parte of reason, and then will he strongly oppresse [f. 64 d] and subdew all the parte of reason, and then is man but a[9] very beest. And at the last[10] he will cast man[11] with all his honor and dignitie into the erremedyable sycknes of extreme ruyon.

What was the cause y[t] Lucifer fell, which was sett in the most honorable dignite y[t] euer was creature y[t] god mad? None other cause but for[12] vsing of Elacion.[13] O this perillous core of this glorious fruite of honorable dignitie. This core in hym[14] wroughte his naturall propertie, which doth[15] eleuate and lyft vp this fruite aboue his proper place and aboue his knolledge, and at last[16] aboue the highest parte of heauen. For the core wold nedes set the fruite of Lucyferes dignitie equall with the goddhed and Lucyfer vngraciously consentyd to the same. But what fell therof? Incontynently

[1] H, Y: "used or touched".
[2] C, Y, H: "elacion or pride". A: "election".
[3] Y, C: "The first coore".   [4] C, H: "have".
[5] C, Y, H: "memory".   [6] C, Y, H: "in".   [7] Omitted in H.
[8] C, Y, H: "and not only aboue his owne proper place but...owne knowledge".
[9] Omitted in C, Y, H.   [10] H: "least".
[11] C, Y, H: "the man".   [12] Omitted in C, H.
[13] C, Y, H: "elacion (Y: delacion) or pride".
[14] Y omits "in hym".   [15] C, Y, H: "did".
[16] C, Y, H: "the last".

Lucyfer, with all his honor and dignitie, discendyth[1] from the highest parte of heaven to the deapest doungion[2] in hell. How wrought this core with our Alterparent[3] Adam, who was in the most honorable dignitie that euer was man, and so highe shall neuer man be sett again of immortalitie and the[4] gretest honor of innocensye? But this core therwith not[5] contentyd wold nedes haue his fruite in an higher pointe, and sett hym at the last so highe y^t he sett hym[6] clerly aboue the reasonable soule of Adam, wherunto He follisshely consentyd, and wold haue [ben][7] aswise as gode. What followyd of hym? Incontynently was he[8] dryven owt of [the][9] heavenly paridize into the vale of mysery and Wretchidnes, Hee lost his dignitie of ymmortalitie and was abhomynable and mortall, He lost his honor of[10] innocensie and was made fraile and synfull. How practysyd this core with the mightie king Pharoo, whose honorable dignitie was so great y^t he was not only king of egipt with many other countries, [f. 65] But he had[11] the subiection and captivitie of the people of god, the childeren of Isararell? But this perillous core wold not thus be satisfied, but nedly wold enhance his fruite, and brought hym[12] so highe[13] that he satt clerely aboue reason and all the partes therof. What fell of yt? Sone after Pharoo was[14] drowned in the bottom of the redd see with all his power and dignitie.

O perillous core y^t brought Lucyfer with[15] all his dignitie owt of the highest parte of heaven into the deapest parte[16] of hell.[17] O perillous core y^t brought Adame with all hys honor and dignitie owt of paradise into the vale of myserie.

[1] C: "discended".   [2] Y: "part".
[3] C: "alter apparant": H: "apparet": Y: "our parent".
[4] C, Y, H: "in the".   [5] C, H: "not therwith".
[6] Y: "them".   [7] C, Y, H.
[8] C, Y, H: "of him (Y: them). Then he was incontinatly".
[9] C, Y, H.   [10] C, Y, H: "and".
[11] C, Y, H insert "with". Y inverts "subiection and captivitie".
[12] Omitted in C, H.
[13] Y: "but immediatly would hang his fruit and bough so high".
[14] C, H: "was not Pharoo...".   [15] H: "and".   [16] C, H: "pit".
[17] Y omits the sentence about Lucifer.

[O perilous core that brought kinge Pharao[1] with all his powre and dignitie into the bottome of the red sea.][2] O perillous core y[t] hast heretofore distroied innumerable kinges and princes, and hast broughte them with ther honorable dignitie vnto ruyon and mysery. O perillous core y[t] woldest in like wise from hensforth vtterly confound all kinges and princes that[3] will thy[4] false appetyte applie or[5] folloo. Wherfore lett euery christen [kinge][6] and prince, and all other persons rewardid with this fruite of honorable dignitie, beware of vnreasonable Elacion and[7] the core therof.

But what shalbe said of the holsom fruite of good example belonging to the Clergie? May so good a fruite haue so bad a core? Yea, Veryly. This fruite hath a subtyll core, and of his proper nature is the[9] distruction of all good workes. It is namyd subtyll glorie or gloriacion. And the vsers of this fruite of good example haue nede to be ware wisely of this core, for be [ye][10] suer this fruite will haue this core. It[11] apperith verie subtyll to the will or vnderstonding of man, and will enter by fyve false or subtyll steppes or he come [f. 65 d] to his resting[12] place.

First this core[13] of glorie will bring a man to remember, and recken in his mynd, the good examples or[14] meritoriouse deedes y[t] he hath done or cawsyd to be don, which semyth to be good rather then ill.[15] But if a man do wisely even there let hym rest; let no man medle with this subtyll and false core,[16] nor with this[17] craftie perswasion. For lett vs be fast and suer y[t] all our good deedes be truly nomberyd, reconyd and[18] rememberid in the eternall boke of [the][19]

Subtile glory or glorificacion .2. core[8]

---

[1] Omitted in H.   [2] C, Y, H.
[3] Y: "and that".   [4] C: "their": H: "the".
[5] Y: "and".   [6] C, Y, H.
[7] Omitted in C, Y, H.
[8] Y, C, H: "the 2ⁿᵈ core of good example".
[9] C, Y, H insert "key and...".   [10] C, Y, H.
[11] C, Y, H: "and it".   [12] C, Y, H: "verie restinge".
[13] Y: "king".   [14] C, Y, H: "and".
[15] Y: "evill".   [16] H: "roote".   [17] C, Y, H: "his".
[18] C, H: "or".   [19] C, Y, H.

eternall knolledge of god, and y^t without omyssion of the least branche or ioynt^1 of them, and there shalbe redy^2 for vs at our nede. Therfore,^3 if we wilbe suer to begile^4 this false core, when he exhortith vs to recon our vertues deedes^5 let vs Busyly recon, nombre and accompt our synnes, and be repentant for them with hope of remyssion. Stop this subtyll core at this pointe, or els he^6 will bring vs to reiose our selves in our good deedes, examples or workes; And this semyth^7 not Verie evill, though it be nether good nor necessarie. For if we will reiose our selves of^8 our good deedes or workes, lett vs reiose only in god and in his grace, wherby and by whome we haue don it, and not in the good deede.^9 For thoughe the doers therof had neuer ben made or creatyd the same good deede should haue ben don. Therfore, when we be provokyd therto, let vs only ioye in god and gyve lawdes to hym y^t gyveth vs grace to do them, and nothing in the deedes. And with that let vs be sorry y^t we haue not performyd our grace in doing many moo good deedes by vs lewdly omyttyd, y^t we ought and nothing haue don. Yf we sett our willes therto By^10 thies menes we shall well reiect hym with his false purpose [at]^11 the second stepp^12 thoughe we dyd yt not at the furst.

If he wynne the^13 stepp on vs and Bring vs in ons to reiose our selves in our [f. 66] good examples or deedes, then he offerith to vs hym self, which is^14 glorie or glorificacion. Y^t is no more but to esteme vs to be happy and^15 vertuous or^16 glorious for doing of the same, and to repute our selves

---

^1 C, Y, H: "pointe".   ^2 C, Y, H: "shall they be".
^3 C, Y, H: "and therfore".   ^4 C, Y, H: "will suerly beguile".
^5 C, H: "of vertuousnes": Y: "our vertuousness".
^6 C, Y, H: "pointe and he will neuer covet or desire vs further. But if we consent to him at this pointe he".
^7 C, Y, H: "seme".   ^8 C, Y, H: "of our self for".
^9 H omits "and not in the good deede".
^10 C, Y, H: "and by".   ^11 C, Y, H. A: "and".
^12 C, Y, H: "this second stop". This form occurs instead of "stepp" throughout this passage in C and H.   ^13 C, Y, H: "this".
^14 C, Y, H: "with his".   ^15 Omitted in C, Y, H.
^16 C, Y, H: "and".

to be belouid[1] people of god, and to be those y[t] kepe the lawes and[2] comaundymentes of god better then other synners doo. Now lett vs beware, and lett[3] vs mightyly resyst hym, for now y[is] false core shewith hym self most vnto vs in his proper nature, spreding his baner openly in a fyld as our mortall ennymie. But lett vs stand styffly ayenst hym, for yet may we withstond hym yf we will. Ther is no better remedy then to consyder if we haue don any good deed or good example yet haue we[4] don nothing so motch as our dewtie is, and of very kindnes we arr bound to do. And then lett vs remember we can neuer worthilie recompense almightie god for his Benifytes, First, for the benyfytes of creacion, the benyfytes of redemption, the benifytes of his preseruacion, with a suer knollege y[t] all we do or haue don[5] is of god; both for[6] the soule and the[7] bodie All commyth of hym and nothing of our selfes. And besydes this to consyder y[t] our[8] vngraciousnes and synfulnes of lyving[9] and vnkind dealing ayenst god comyth only of our vnhappie and froward dispocicion, and thies two pointes well consyderyd with our owne fylthynes, shall rather cawse vs vtterly to[10] dispice our self then glorie in our self.

Howbeit, yf this false and subtyll core, with his third stepp or Bulwark vpon vs, begyn and bringith vs[11] ones in y[t] point y[t] we glorifie vs in our selfe for our good deedes, Then will he make a strong sawte[12] to wyn [f. 66d] the iiij[th] stepp or ward vpon vs, and [that][13] is to esteme our self to be worthie to be glorified byyond all other persons, and y[t] other men shall repute vs to be vertuous and good folkes and the charitable kepers of the Lawes of god. And to thentent y[t] he will suerly and strongly[14] wyn y[is] ward He will prouoke vs to do suche good deedes as we will do in the

[1] C, Y, H: "the beloved".   [2] C, H omit "lawes and".
[3] C, Y, H: "nowe let".   [4] C, Y, H: "we have".
[5] C, Y, H: "have don or do".   [6] Omitted in C, Y, H.
[7] Omitted in C and Y.   [8] C, Y, H: "all our".
[9] C, Y, H: "sinfull Lyvinges".   [10] C, H: "shall cause vs rather to".
[11] C, H: "and take holde on vs". In C written later in a blank space.
[12] C, Y. H: "assault".   [13] C, Y, H.   [14] Y: "straightly".

face of ye world, y^{t1} is, to [doe]^2 them in such maner y^t people^3 may know it^4 for our deedes. How so euer we wooll in doing our devocions, beit praier, fasting or almes deede,^{5} rather [do them] in open places then in private: otherwhiles, when^6 we haue don them righte secretly, to shew them vttward to other folkes, and so to make them tappere, or^7 at the leest to be well contentyd y^t other shall declare or manyfest them: And at the last be glad to here the praises therof. Or els yf^8 we doo any charitable or meritorious deedes we will cawse scutchions,^{9} Badges or scriptures, or both, to be made to declare openly the doers therof. But we will saie, for our excuse, yt shalbe a good occasion for^{10} other y^t herafter shall see or here therof to praie the rather for there soules. O false elusyon of this subtiltie!^{11} Let vs Be suer y^{t12} all this open declaracions for any good deedes do vtterly destroy our merites for them, or at the leest yt profyteth nothing to^{13} our soules. When so euer we do any good or meritoriouse deedes^{14} let vs do yt with the perfect syrcumstance, which is only for charitie And in the honor of god. The Auctor should^{15} nether devise scowcher^{16} nor scripture, for god, which is the trew sercher of all hartes, he^{17} is the large rewarder of all good deedes and [f. 67] intentes, and rewardith all persons of euery good intent or act that is don more then he deseruith. Therfore if our actes be well orderid it is but a^{18} vanytie to add therto other knolledge then the only [knowledge]^{19} of god, for it sufficeth^{20} and neuer failyth. But [if] our intentes be vpon

---

^{1} Y: "then". $\qquad$ ^{2} C, Y, H.
^{3} C, H: "all people": Y: "all the people".
^{4} Omitted in H. $\qquad$ ^{5} H, Y: "deeds".
^{6} H: "while". $\qquad$ ^{7} C: "or els".
^{8} Omitted in C, H.
^{9} Blank space in C, H: omitted in Y.
^{10} C, H: "to". $\qquad$ ^{11} C, Y, H: "subtill core".
^{12} Omitted in C, Y, H. $\qquad$ ^{13} H, Y: "for".
^{14} C, Y: "deede". $\qquad$ ^{15} H: "shall".
^{16} Blank space in C, H: Y: "scutches".
^{17} Omitted in C, Y, H. $\qquad$ ^{18} Omitted in C.
^{19} C, Y, H. $\qquad$ ^{20} C, Y, H: "which sufficeth".

this open¹ knolledge, yᵗ besydes our merite to god yet we wold gladly haue some laude or good reporte of the people for our doing therof, Lett vs then be suer our merites be clerly lost; yet is the dede good and we haue taken therfore our owne reward, which is the lawde and fame of the people. Let euery man examyn thuttermost of his owne mynd and intent when he settyth vpon suche² open knolledge of his good deedes, Whether ther be no parte of his purpose to haue some fame or lawde therfor.

But this malicyous core³ in the iiijᵗʰ stepp or point will not be so content, yᵗ is, to make vs⁴ vtterly to lose all our merytes of our good examples⁵ and deedes, and also in the same to cawse vs mortally to synne. And yᵗ is thus, when at his desier we make any suche knolledge openly⁶ of our good workes he will not only entice vs to desier therfore lawde or⁷ pompe of the people but inducyth vs to think our selves for suche actes worthie to be lawdyd and glorified of the people. And, if he can bring vs yᵉʳ to, then hath he won the iiijᵗʰ warde, for yᵗ is a depe mortall synne, and the verye synne of vayne glorie.

The best defence for suche assente⁸ to this point shalbe to vs to remember, when we be sturryd to think our selfes worthie to be gloryefyed of other folkes for our good dedes, How abhomynable we be of our synnes, both in deede and thoughte.⁹ And if we will nedes shew our good deedes to be gloryfyed for them lett vs shew the Bad also, and so both togethers, for yᵗ is an indyfferent waie, and then let vs se well our selfes how mutche worthie we be to be glorified. Peraduenture if we should thus do, as glorious as we wold be, we wold¹⁰ be righte loth to shew our faces for shame. Besydes this, lett vs think for a suertie, when so euer and as

---

¹ C, Y, H: "our open".   ² C, Y, H: "any such".
³ Omitted in H.   ⁴ Omitted in C, H.
⁵ C, Y, H: "for our good example".
⁶ C, Y, H: "open knowledge".   ⁷ H, Y: "and".
⁸ "as sente" in A.
⁹ C, Y, H: "thought and deed".
¹⁰ H: "should".

often as we be of desier or of appetyte therto, we[1] intend
[f. 67 d] the most dishonour to god our creator and redemor
ther[2] lieth in vs to do, for we wold haue y[t] don to vs that
only[3] to his godhed apperteynith, For he is he to[4] whom
thankes for[5] all good dedes should be don. Also euery
creature by thorder of humylitie, though he do neuer so
many good deedes, should repute hym self most wretchid,
and not only that, but also[6] should inwardly desier to be
[so] reputyd with all other people.

Yet[7] this dampnable and curssyd core will not be thus
satisfyed to leve vs in this greate danger of mortall synne,
but will also wynne on vs the fyfth and last[8] step without[9]
we resyst hym mightylie,[10] for his nature is suche the more
he wynneth in[11] vs the more strong[12] he is, and we the weker.
The fyfth stepp is y[t] he woll[13] cawse our selfes to think [our
selves] to be [so] glorious in our vertue and in our good
deedes y[t] the glorie of our selfes and the glorie of all other
people suffycith not for vs, but y[t] we be[14] worthie to be
glorified of god. O false, cancoryd, rotten[15] coore, what
meanest thou y[t] thou woldest haue vs, wretchid synners,
testeme our selfes worthie to[16] haue y[t] reward y[t] all the
virgyns, martyrs and confessors, nor the holyest saintes in
heaven, could neuer deserue? Woldest thou haue vs,
dampnable creatures, to presume or thynk vs worthie, or of
dignitie,[17] to haue y[t] reward y[t] the sacrid virgyn of glorie[18]
could neuer think hur self worthie to haue or optein? For y[t]
reward to be glorified is[19] so highe y[t] neuer man or[20] woman

---

[1] C, Y, H: "desire of (H: for) our appetite, we...".
[2] C, H: "that".   [3] Omitted in Y.
[4] C, H: "he it is to": Y: "he is to".
[5] C, Y, H: "the glorie for (Y: of)".
[6] H omits "but also".   [7] H: "yea".
[8] C, Y, H: "the last".   [9] Y: "except".
[10] C, Y, H: "right mightely".   [11] C, Y, H: "on".
[12] C, Y: "stronger".   [13] C, H: "would".
[14] Omitted in C, H.   [15] Omitted in C, Y, H.   [16] C, H: "for to".
[17] C, Y, H: "thinke or presume vs worthie of our dignitie".
[18] Blank space for "of glorie" in C, H. Y: "virgines glory".
[19] C, H: "It is".   [20] C, Y, H: "nor".

could truly saie he deseruith[1] it; But only christ Iesu for y^t that he was god.[2] Wherfor lett not the best of vs synners think any other worthynes in our selfes But to be perpetually tormentyd of our gostly ennymie the Devill, and not to be glorified [of][3] god, saving by the great infynit[4] Marcy of our maker and redemor. And this to remember oftentymes [f. 68] in our myndes shall not be the worst remedy ayenst the venemeouse core in this fyfth stepp or point,[5] for the rather we dele with hym the easier he is to be withstandid,[6] and worst at the last. This is the pestiferous[7] core of this holsome fruite of good example and of all other good workes don by any person, spirituall or temporall, And the better work it is, and the more profytt to the doers, the more busie[8] will this malicious core be. Therfore, my lordes and masters of the Clergie, when ye vse your fruite be ye well ware of the core and toche it not. Yet throw it not awaie, but lett your poore chamberlein kepe it for some other purpose, as[9] it may be necessarie.

What then is the core of worldly prosperitie, the fruite of the Chyvalrie? It is vaine delectacion, a core righte dangerous with that fruite to be vsyd. The propertie of this [core][11] is not only to alienate[12] clerely the mynd of man from god and good vertues,[13] and also from hym self, but therto to involve obtusely[14] the memorie and vnderstonding of man, and fynallie to make man abuse hym self, both in bodie and soule, and then folowith[15] greate aduersyte and

Vaine delectation
3. core[10]

---

[1] C, Y, H: "deserved".
[2] C, Y, H: "for he was that that was onelie god".
[3] C, Y, H.
[4] C, H: "great favor and". C written in later in a blank space.
[5] C, Y, H: "fifte (Y: first) stoppe or pointe, but in anie wise let vs resist him ere he come (Y: beginn) at this pointe".
[6] C, Y, H: "to withstand".   [7] C, Y, H: "pestilingall".
[8] Omitted in H.   [9] Omitted in C, Y, H.
[10] H, C: "3. core".   [11] C, Y, H.
[12] H: "bereave". In C "bereve" has been written in later.
[13] C, Y, H: "vertuousnes".
[14] C, Y, H: "thereto involve securely (Y: obtusely)".
[15] Y: "folow".

vtter distruction. Vaine delectacion is properly when a man settyth his loue greatly or howgely[1] on a thing. And if[2] a man ons enter into y[is] delectacion in[3] worldly prosperite the more he enterith therin the more delyte he shalhaue therof, and at the last shall sett all[4] his whole mynd theron, even like[5] as though his mynd were ordenyd for the same[6] purpose only and for none other thing, and so shall his mynd be clerly alienate[7] from god and hym self, and at the last abuse the man both in bodie and in[8] soule, as hath[9] ben said, and so [f. 68 d] fynallie to distroie hym.

First to prove [that] if this faillible core of Vain delectacion be found[10] or sett in worldly prosperitie it will clerely with-drawe and alienat a mans mynd from god and hym self. Wherfore yt is best for[11] euery man to[12] examen hym self, and so shall he best know how greatly[13] his mynd is in a maner ravisshed when he settyth his delectacion in[14] worldly prosperitie. Shalhe not[15] be in y[t] case [that][16] at mattens and masse his mynd will runne theron, and, as I wene, he doth nether eate nor drink but his mynd wilbe there, and often-tymes let men from there slepe[17] and other naturall restes. And for conclusion,[18] let the bodie be wheare yt will, or do what it pleasith,[19] the mynd wilbe there. And thus perillous delectacion of worldly prosperitie will not faile to bring with hur the haste abusion and distruction of man, And two[20] ennymies, in a maner as ill[21] as hur self, which be concupisence and delectacion of the fleasshe, and pride[22] of the lyfe.

[1] C, H: "knowledge": Y: "knowledge over...".
[2] C, Y, H: "then if".   [3] C, H: "his delectacion of...".
[4] Omitted in C, Y, H.   [5] C, Y, H: "likewise".
[6] Y: "self same".   [7] C, Y, H: "aliened".
[8] Omitted in H.   [9] Blank space in C, H.
[10] C, Y, H: "fixed".   [11] Omitted in C, Y, H.
[12] Omitted in Y.   [13] Omitted in Y.
[14] C, H: "on".   [15] C, H: "shall not he".   [16] C, Y, H.
[17] C, Y, H: "thereon and all in vaine shall he eate or drinke but that they will be there, and often tymes let man from his sleepe".
[18] C, Y, H: "a true conclusion".
[19] C, Y, H: "he will...he pleasith".   [20] C, Y: "twoe other".
[21] C, Y, H: "as well".   [22] C, Y, H: "of pride".

This Delectacion, which[1] is the fowle lust of the fleasshe, and the delectacion[2] of the world ar[3] mutch like in condicions, aswell in the alyenacion of [the][4] mynd in maner[5] as otherwise tabuse hym to his owne distruction. But yet this delectacion of the world is the worst,[6] for as to refrain fleashely delectacion ther be dyuerse thinges yᵗ will somewhat slake yt, But for this delectacion of the world ther is almost no remedie. For the delectacion of the fleasshe a man may watche, fast long, or kepe slender[7] diatt yᵗ yt shall not greatly truble hym: to the other it will nothing prevaile. For the fleasshe, if[8] yt be a man yᵗ may marie, let hym take a wife: he may vse hur so that percase he shalhaue no greate delectacion nether in hur nor in any[9] other, and the yong weddyd wyves for see[10] not greatly to bring ther husbandes into [f. 69] yᵗ case.[11] It is but a folie to fulfill there appetites. Better it were the wif to lack a tyme, or[12] twentie, then the husband to be comberyd with a quartance by one[13] year or two, and speciallie if it come yᵗ waie it [is][14] perillous [to][14] cure.

But suche a medicene will not help thother[15] delectacion, for yᵉ more of yᵗ insaciable core a man takith the more he delytyth, And [if][16] it were possyble for[17] hym to haue all thys world yt wold skant quentche his thurst. How folishe or how madd is man yᵗ will thus mutche delighte in his mortall ennymie. This[18] is the ennymie of all ennymies yᵗ will not be content to eleuate the mynd of man clerly from god and hym self, And to sett it only and intierly in corruptible and transytorie vanytie, as is before rehersid, and

---

[1] Omitted in C, Y, H.
[2] C, Y, H: "flesh or body and dilectacion".
[3] Omitted in C, Y, H.   [4] C, Y, H.
[5] C omits "in maner".   [6] C, Y, H: "worse".
[7] C, Y, H: "soe slender".   [8] C, Y, H: "prevaile. Or els, if".
[9] C, Y: "none".   [10] C, H: "force".
[11] Y: "place".   [12] C, Y, H: "waste a sigh or".
[13] C, Y, H: "a quarten by a". [14] C, Y, H.
[15] C, Y, H: "to thother".   [16] C, Y, H.
[17] Omitted in C, H.   [18] C, Y, H: "for this".

also will involve and wrapp bothe the memorie and vnder-
standing of man¹ to the condicions and properties of an
vnreasonable beest, and to make them self as an horsse or a
moile,² the which thing in man to be don or made holy
king³ David forbydith of all thinges, for of yᵗ insaciabilitie
followith a Beastly ponyshement.

Yet this cruell ennymie, the core of vnreasonable delectacion, will not be satisfied to haue the man in⁴ bodie as a
beast, and for yᵗ to suffer beastly ponysshement, but ouer
yᵗ will not rest tyll he bring aswell the soule as the bodie⁵
to the most extreme confusion and distrucion; therfore⁶ this
delectacion may well and truly be callid a beastly appetite.

How may it be provid yᵗ this beastly appetite of delectacion involveth and wrappeth thunderstonding and memorie
of man, thie being ij partes of the reasonable soule? Yes,
veryly, this delectacion of worldly prosperitie, with thelp
[of]⁷ his two redie adherentes, which be [f. 69 d] delectacion
of the fleasshe and pride of Lyeff,⁸ will so involve and wrapp
his vnderstonding and memorie, which is the knollege or
rememberance of man, that he shall nether know nor remember god nor man, nor yet⁹ hym self as he ought, but
be¹⁰ as a thing yᵗ hath clerly lost all knolledge and rememberance. He shall not know god with honor to be the¹¹ gyver
and the¹² withdrawer of all prosperitie at his highe will,¹³
But rather he will think yt comyth to hym by righte off
sucession, or by desertes of his owne wisdome, hardenes,

---

¹ C, Y, H: "afore rehearsed, But that will (Y inserts "both" here
instead of after "wrap") involve and wrap the memory and the vnder-
standing of man, And at the last soe abuse himself from the condicions
of a reasonable man".   ² H: "and a mule". Y: "mule".
³ H inserts "or done" again, then C, Y, H continue "the holy
Kinge".   ⁴ C, Y, H: "made in".
⁵ C, Y, H: "the bodie as the Soule".
⁶ C, Y, H: "destruccion and confusion·and therefore".
⁷ C, Y, H.   ⁸ C, Y, H: "the lief".
⁹ Omitted in C, Y, H.   ¹⁰ C, Y, H: "to be".
¹¹ Y: "bothe the".   ¹² Omitted in C, H.
¹³ C, H: "good…". In C "good" has been written in later but part
of the blank space remains as in H.

strengith or connyng. He will not know me[n]¹ with
reuerence or dewtie, for he will esteme hym self to be more
worthie then other, or at the leest to be fellow with his
Better.² He will not knowe nor remember hym self,³
from whence he cam, what he is, nor whether he⁴ shall
[go].⁵ All we cam of Adam, and which of vs, the prince
or the poore, is⁶ next of kynne by grace to the manhod, or
which ys most noble, yt is hard to tell. But either we wilbe
so lothe to know and remember from whens we⁷ cam yᵗ
we in nowise wilbe knowne⁸ of our grandfather or grand-
mother, or els we wilbe lothe to medle with any man yᵗ
knowith them, and peraduenture even so by our fathers and
mothers, and other of our nere⁹ kynne. Thus we will not
know from whens we come.¹⁰

Do we not also forgett what we be, and speciallie when
we delyte in this vnhappie fruite? Who will know hym self
in prosperite what thing he is in deede? For all his prosperitie what is he better yᵉⁿ¹¹ a mysarable man, hauing and
suffering all the passions, disseases¹² and infyrmities, aswell
of the soule as of the bodie, equall [with]¹³ the poore plough-
man, and oftentymes mutche worsse. Will any of thies
diseases, [f. 70] passions or infyrmities forebere hym any
moment¹⁴ of an hower for all his worldly prosperite, or
what beast, fowle or fysshe will obey [him]¹⁵ more therfore,
or what beast or worme in his furie will forbere hym more
then the poorest begger yᵗ goith? Loke when our glorious
garmentes be don off, and we nakyd, what differens is then
betwene vs and the poore laborers. Peraduenture a more¹⁶

---

¹ C, Y, H.   ² H: "betters".
³ C, Y, H: "knowe himself neither remember".
⁴ C: "it".
⁵ C, Y, H omit a verb and insert: "Whence we came".
⁶ C, H: "or": Y: "of".   ⁷ C, H: "it".
⁸ C, H: "noe wise (H: wayes) would be knowne". Y: "we would in
nowise be known".   ⁹ Omitted in C, H.
¹⁰ C, Y, H: "came".   ¹¹ C, Y, H: "the better but".
¹² Y: "and all the diseases".   ¹³ C, Y, H.
¹⁴ C, Y, H: "one mynute".   ¹⁵ C, Y, H.
¹⁶ "a more" joined in A.

foolle and shamefull karcase. Also loke whether our naturall
mother brought vs not into this world[1] with like sorrowes
and paines, and the symple bodie all nakyd, as the child of
povertie and myserie. Loke a litle furder in[2] our selfes;
loke in[2] our fylthie thinges y[t] righte naturally from our
fylthie bodies doth come.[3] In prosperite peraduenture it is
more abhomynable then of the poore pilgreme. Thies
thinges men will not [know] in them selfes.[4] He wold be
lothe to here or[5] know what he was xx[te] yeres past.[6]
Thus men haue forgotten from whens thei cam and what
thei be.

Will thei remember whether thei shall [go]? I wold to
god thei wold, for that mighte fortune them to amend the
resydew. Howbeit, whether thei remember or not, deth
comyth and tarieth not. How sone,[7] or in what maner, or
in what place, yt is[8] not knowne, for, where man reconith
and trustith to contynew xx[te] or xxx[te9] yeres, death comyth
oftetymes in fortie daies or lesse, and when he comyth all
the treasure in the tower can not intreate hym for one daie.
In what maner will he come as thou wynest? Thou trustist
he will come with curtuous demeanure, or with respect at
thy pleasure. He wold come[10] oftentymes cruellie and
[f. 70d] faruently, with a sherp pestilens, or with a short
pluresys, or a stitche or[11] impostume, and the man shalbe
hole this nighte and deedd to morrow, or in to or thre daies,[12]
and y[t] is long leasure. Many maner of diuersities are[13]

[1] C, Y, H: "brought vs into this wretched world".
[2] C, Y, H: "on".
[3] C, Y, H: "that goeth naturallie from our filthie body".
[4] C, H: "knowe in (H: of) themselves amonge".
[5] Y omits "here or".
[6] C, Y, H add "or lesse".
[7] C, Y, H: "how so".   [8] C, H: "is it".
[9] C, Y, H: "xx thirtie or fortie".
[10] C, Y, H: "In what manner will he come, there as a man trusteth he will come with some cortesie or respite, he will come".
[11] Blank space in C. H: "…and an…". Y: "tech and an…".
[12] C, Y, H: "or in three daies oftentimes".
[13] Omitted in C, Y, H.

therin, y[t] in maner it is impossible to recon them to execute[1]
ther experiens vnto you. And as to the place where he will
execute this[2] deede he will not shew it but kepe yt secrete.[3]
For men trusting to die in ther beddes in good prosperitie
oftetymes die by[4] execution, and not worth a penny; otherwhiles in prison, in [a][5] deepe doungeon, And ofttymes
ther[6] superfluous prosperities be the cause and not ther[7]
gylt. Otherwhiles [are some] slaine in the feildes, or in[8]
the waie, or in some other place by ennymies[9] or theves;
otherwhiles soddenly[10] killid in some other place, and y[t]
by them in whom thei[11] trustyd righte well, by casualtie
y[t] no man wold[12] recon. But for a suertie, as theis[13] waies be
innumerable so be his places, and so thend of all prosperous
folkes is vnknowne, and withowt doubt more vncerten
then thend of a poore man.

Yet loke a litle farder on our[14] selfes. When we be dede,
for all pompe[15] and prosperite, what is our presious karcase,
arid what shall we haue hense with vs? Is our karcase[16] any
thing but a caryon most vile and abhomynable? And thoughe
ther be laid abowt it sylkes[17] and seldalles,[18] with balme[19] and
spices, to the valew of a m[ll] [li],[20] Yet it is[21] none other
thing[22] but rotten[23] dong and dogges will not eate yt, and the
laser[24] werre there but as one of vs. What should[25] we carie

---

[1] H, Y: "that in them to execute...". C: "that in a man it is impossible to reckon. Then to reckon them to execute".
[2] C, Y, H: "his".   [3] C, Y, H: "secretly".
[4] C, Y, H: "in prosperitie and often (H: many) tymes he dieth
by".   [5] C, Y, H: "and in a".
[6] C, Y, H: "his".   [7] C, H: "the": Y: "his".
[8] C, Y, H: "on".   [9] C, Y, H: "his enemyes".
[10] Omitted in Y.   [11] C, Y, H: "them whom he".
[12] C, Y, H: "will".   [13] C, H: "his".
[14] C, H: "your".   [15] C, H: "our pompe".
[16] C, H omit "and what...our karcase".
[17] H: "laid out about sylkes". C, Y also omit "it", but otherwise
follow A.   [18] C, H have blank space: Y: "fynealls".
[19] C, H: blank: Y: "lawn".   [20] C, Y: H: "hundred pound".
[21] C, H: "is it".   [22] Omitted in H.
[23] C, Y, H: "a rotten".   [24] Blank space in C, H. Y: "last".
[25] C, Y, H: "shall".

hens with vs? Nether regaltie, pompe, prosperitie, nor earthly thing,[1] for nakid we cam and nakid [f. 71] we shall depart[2] hens, Even as the poorest soule y^t euer beggyd brede. And [as][3] for our good deedes, we shall not nede to carie them with vs, for thei be truly notyd before god or our spirite[4] be departyd. And thus doth vngraciouse delectacions[5] involve and wrapp[6] so our vnderstonding and memorie y^t nether we know, nor wyll not[7] know, god, our neighebor, or our selves.

And ouer this he will make man to abuse hym self and to follow the condicions and properties of a brute beast, as a horsse or a moile,[8] and to forsake the condicions and properties of a man. Yf he sett ones his delectacion[9] to haue thies worldly prosperities[10] He shalbe so gredy and desiorous[11] to them y^t he forcyth not what pain or labor he takyth or doith to haue them, And ouer y^t, foreseeth not how shamfully or how vntruly he cometh by them. So he may haue them he lokyth nether[12] to the feere of [god],[13] the shame of the world, nor y^t which ensuyth or followith, but lokyth all only tobteyne his desier, And this is the verie naturall condicion[14] of a horsse or a moile, or of any other vnreasonable beest, for thei regard nothing els But thobtenyng of ther purpose and delyttes. And at some tymes he shalbe in a transe[15] or museis y^t he shall[16] nether tell perfectly [what he seeth],[17] what he hearith or what he spekyth.

---

[1] C, Y, H: "none (Y: or any) earthlie thing els".

[2] Y: "return".   [3] C, Y, H.   [4] H: "spirits".

[5] C, H: "doe our gracious delectacion": Y: "doth our vngracious delectacion".

[6] H: "enwrap".   [7] Omitted in C, Y, H.

[8] C, Y, H read "mule" for "moile" throughout this passage.

[9] "his delectacion" omitted in H.

[10] C, Y: "this worldlie prosperitie".

[11] C, Y, H: "soe desirous".   [12] C, Y, H: "not neither".

[13] C, Y, H. In A: "good".

[14] C, H: "desire condicion or propertie": Y: "condicion or propertie".

[15] C, Y, H: "at seasons he shalbe in (Y: at) such traunce".

[16] Y: "can".   [17] C, H (Y: saith).

Then he[1] is a verie beest, or worsse then a beest, when theis worldly prosperities be obteynid. Then is [the][2] man a ferd to go from them, and thinkith y^t euery man will haue them [f. 71 d] from hym. And he abusyth hym self not only in[3] this false delight of coueting them But also he[4] will abuse hym self mutche more in the vnreasonable delighte in thuse and keping of them. But how beastly is he made if it fortune hym to forgoo them by chaunce of the world or otherwise. Then is he in suche a sorrofull being[5] y^t therbye he goith madd for sorroo, and suddenly will murmure[6] ayenst god; [and] some for sorrow[7] kill them selfes. This is a sorrofull lyffe[8] aboue all beastly sorrowes. Now behold well whether this delectacion do[9] not sore abuse man, insomotche as[10] he is made therby a[11] beest, And oftentymes wursse[12] then all this. For his will and purpose is to bring the man, both bodie and soule, to vtter[13] distruction and confusion if he folloo yt, withowt the greate mercy of god.

Behold the greate king Nabugodonyser y^t was in asmotche worldly prosperitie as any man mighte be; but at the last he sett his delectacion somutche therin y^t he nether knew[14] god nor hym self, But vtterly followid his vnreasonable desier and[15] delyght, And so abusyd hym self in beastly condicions tyll at the last he was vtterly deposyd from all his prosperite, and driven owt emongist beest[es].[16] And ther emongist them fedd like a best by a long season, tyll at the last he rememberid his old beastly and vnreasonable delectacion, and then he estemyd hym self more worthie to be

[1] Y: "his".   [2] C, Y, H.
[3] C, Y, H: "not him self in".
[4] C, Y, H: "in covetinge of them, But he".
[5] C, Y, H: "agony".
[6] C, Y, H: "and soe die for sorrowe and murmour".
[7] C, Y, H: "for sorrow some".
[8] C: "lowe"; H: blank; Y: "love".   [9] C, Y, H: "doth".
[10] Omitted in C, Y, H.   [11] C, Y, H: "as a".
[12] C, Y, H add: "yet the properties of this vngracious delectacion is much worse".   [13] C, H: "the vtter".
[14] C, H: "theron that he knewe neither". Y follows A until "knewe neither".   [15] C, Y, H: omit "desier and".   [16] C: "beastes".

[f. 72] a beest then a king or a[1] knighte, and with a great
sorrow and humble repentance and hevines that he toke
towardes god he was restoryd to his kingdom and obteynid[2]
it again. But lett vs not trust one[3] suche a speciall grace, but
somewhat remember Nero, the great, prosperous Emperor,
yᵗ followid so farr the delectacions[4] of his beastly appetytes[4]
that, when he perseivid [him self] to be distroyed or ponished
therfore, He vtterly slew hym self, and so was distroid both
bodie and soule. How wrought this[5] delectacion with the
most prosperous and wyse[6] Salamon? Did not he therby
forsake his god, his creatore, and[7] did Idolytre? How
mutche was Sampson and other prosperous men abusyd by
this perillous core of delectacion. The noble knighte,[8]
Theophilus, for the delyte of worldly prosperytie gave hym
self to the devill. What abusyon was this! Howbeit he was
savid by speciall[9] myracle of our Blyssyd Lady! Wherfore
was the greate Citie of[10] Ierusalem distroied? For ther[11]
delectacion. Wherfore were the greate Cities of Sodoma
and Gomera soncken?[12] For ther abusiall[13] of beestly and
vnreasonable delectacion. Wherfor, all ye noble and prosperous men of the Chyvalrie, sett not your delectacion
therin. I say not yᵗ ye shall forsake or refuse worldly prosperitie, but yᵗ righte well ye may[14] accept it as god and your
prince gyveth it to you. But loke [that] ye neuer delyte
therin, for if ye do yt will accomber[15] you, as it[16] is before
rehersyd. Wherfore this core of your prosperitie is vtterly
to be refusyd by you and all[17] yᵗ enter into worldly pro-

---

[1] Omitted in C, Y, H.

[2] Y: "received".   [3] C, Y, H: "let not vs trust of".

[4] C, H use singular.   [5] H: "his".

[6] C, H: "the prosperous and wiseman". Y follows A save for
"wiseman".   [7] C, Y, H: "verie god and".

[8] H: "king".   [9] Y: "spirituall".   [10] Omitted in C, H.

[11] C, Y, H: "by ponishment for beastlie (Y omits adjective)".

[12] C, H leave blank space: Y: "sounck".

[13] C, Y, H: "but a ponishment for their abusion".

[14] C, Y, H: "I say ye shall not forsake...but ye may right well".

[15] C, Y: "shall comber": H: "shall encumber".

[16] Y ends here.   [17] C: "all other".

speritie. Yet [f. 72d] cast not away this core of delectacioń.
Let your treasury sufficiently kepe it vnto the tyme it[1] may
be better occupied.

Now, ye good commyners, y[t] haue the fruite of tran- Lewd
quilitie, your fruite hath a core of the which ye haue greate enterprise
nede to be ware, for yt hath greuid you many tymes, And 4. core[2]
y[t] marvilously.[3] The core of your fruite is callid lewd
enterprise. I tell you, all beit yt be delicious and plesaunt
to behold, yt is a morsell nothing mete for your diatt. And
if you will nedes deale therwith yt will not only bring you
from tranquilite to the disease of greavous thraldome and
myserie, but also oftentymes to vtter desolacion.[4]

This lewd core of enterprise,[5] or he come to do his sham-
full feete or entent, most comenly he sendith too purssy-
fauntes or messengers before hym, chosen of the worst
for our profytt. The furst of the[6] two messengers is dis-
contentacion or murmurr. This messenger will induce you
to grudge or to make[7] some inward displeasure in doing
your Dewtie, as in paing your farme[8] rentes for howses
and landes to them that ye be bound to pay, or to do some[9]
other particuler seruice y[t] to your tenementes[10] belongith
to do, or to murmur at paymentes[11] of taxes or quindicimes[12]
when thei be grauntyd for cawses necessarie. He will also
induce you to grudge or disdain to be in suche obediens or
subiection to your supperiors or betters.[13] Beware of this
messenger, for he must fetche[14] to you your owne mischef
yf ye to him consent.

And if ye [f. 73] reuerently receive this felloo then[15]

---

[1] H: "that".   [2] H, C: "4th core".
[3] C, H: "right mervelouslie".   [4] H: "destruction".
[5] C, H: "core enterpriseth".   [6] C, H: "theis".
[7] C, H: "or take".   [8] C, H: "farmes".
[9] C, H: "to paye it or for some...".
[10] C, H: "tenauntes". In A "tenauntes" has been erased.
[11] C, H: "the payment".   [12] C, H: "fyfteenes".
[13] H: "and subjects...and betters".
[14] C, H leave blank space, for "fetche", then "you to your...".
[15] C, H: "and reuerently...this fellowe that...".

commyth the second messenger, in a gay, guilt cote, to enveigle your synne[1] with pryde, the most perillous spectakle y[t] the commynaltie may vse. Fowle is it[2] in all men but worst in the poorest. The name of the second messenger is callid[3] Arrogancy, nighe cosen to pride. [H]is very nature[4] and propertie is to entise you[5] to enhable your selves to such thinges as nothing besemeth you[6] to do, suche thinges as you nothing can skill on.[7] He will shew you y[t] ye be made of the same metell and mold[8] y[t] the gentiles be made of. Whie then should thei sport and play and you labor and till?[9] He will tell you also y[t] at your birthes and at[10] your deethes your riches be[11] indifferent. Whie should thei haue somotche of the prosperite and treasure of this world and ye so lytle? Besydes y[t], he will tell you y[t] ye be the childeren and righte enheritors to Adam aswell as thei. Whie should thei haue this great honours,[12] royall castelles and manners, with somotche landes and possessions, and ye but poore cottygees and tenementes?[13] He will shew also how y[t] christ bought you as derely as the nobles with[14] one maner of price, which was his preciouse Bloude. Whie then should ye be of so poore estate and thei of highe[15] degre, or whie should you do them so motche honour and reuerence with chroching and knelyng, and thei take it so highely[16] and stately on them? And percase he will enforme you how conserning[17] your soules and theres, which make[18] you all to be men [f. 73 d] or[19] els ye were all but beestes,[20] god creatyd in you one maner of noblenes without any diuersitie,[21]

Arrogancie

---

[1] Blank space left for "your synne" in C, H.
[2] C, H: "Full ill it is".   [3] Omitted in C, H.
[4] C, H: "His nature".   [5] Omitted in C, H.
[6] C, H: "or".   [7] H: "of".
[8] C, H: "moulde and mettall".   [9] H: "toile".
[10] Omitted in H.   [11] C, H: "is".
[12] C, H: "honour".   [13] C, H: "tenementes and cotages".
[14] C, H: "shew you also whie that Christ bought as derely you as them and with".   [15] C, H: "soe highe".
[16] C, H: "highe".   [17] Omitted in C, H.
[18] C, H: "maketh".   [19] C, H: "for".
[20] C, H: add "wherby".   [21] C, H: "aduersity".

and y^t your soules be as precious to god as theires. Whye then should thei haue of you so greate auctoritie and power to commytt you to prison, and ponishe and iudge[1] you?

But, ye good comyners, in any wise vtterly refuse theis messengers, for, thoughe thei shew the trewith to you, thei meane[2] full falsely, as afterward ye shall well knowe. And, yf ye ones savor of[3] theis thinges, then comyth your lewde enterprise, the core of your fruite of tranquilitie, and he will you encorage to play the men,[4] and byd you remember well the monstracions and[5] shewinges of this messenger,[6] arrogancie. He will byd you to[7] leave to employe your selfes[8] to be subdewid of your felloes; he will promisse to sett you on highe, and to be lordes and gouerners, and no longer to be chorles as ye were before; at[9] the leest he will promysse you to make you[10] fellooes in bodies as god made you in soules, and then ther shalbe[11] a royall rule in this realme. And to put you in furder[12] comfort he will assuer you y^t some of the chyvalrie will take parte openly or priuely, or els at[13] the leest to gyve you sufferance, prove as ye may.

He will also displaie vnto you his banner of Insurrection, and say:[14] "Now sett forward, y^{er} tyme is righte good". But woo be [vnto][15] y^t man y^t will fight ther vnder. He will promisse you to want no treasure to performe your purpose, For he will say: "Some of the clergie will comfort you right well and largely with mony, for thei haue herefor[16] many a daie. The marchantes [f. 74] and fermors, and the[17] graisiers y^t be riche, into this markett will bring there bagges y^t thei haue kept so long. And asfor thold wydowes and

----

[1] C, H: "to commyt to prison, to ponishe and to Iudge you".
[2] C, H: "he shewe...he meaneth".   [3] C, H: "in".
[4] C, H: "man".   [5] C, H: "or".
[6] C, H: "the messengers".   [7] Omitted in C.
[8] C, H add "to labour and to till like beastes nor (H: and) suffer your selfes".   [9] C, H: "or at".   [10] Omitted by H.
[11] C, H: "shall there be...".   [12] C, H: "a further".
[13] C, H: "youre parte openly and privilie, or at".
[14] C, H add "to you".   [15] C, H.
[16] C, H: "looked therefore".
[17] C, H: "the merchantes, the farmors, the".

wyves,[1] [thei] also will ransake ther forsers and there knottyd cloutes to the last penny thei[2] can fynd, and, rather then faile, ther girdles, there beedes and there wedding rignes Thus wisely thei will them bestowe." And asfor men, He promysyth you innumerable.

Yet, ye good comyners, for your owne eas dele not with this false core, but be contentyd with the fruite of tranquilitie: it is for you both profytable and good, and will make you welthie yf welth may be sufferyd. Grudge[3] not agenst your superiors for doing your dewtie: covet not the prosperite of [the][4] Chyvalrie, nor muse not theron: disdain not[5] the greate power of your[6] souuereigne, but with a[7] dew reuerence obey yt, For be ye suer, the highe prouidens of god is [that][8] you should so do,[9] as he declaryth hym self righte plainly to his chosen people when thei desierid a king. Therfore mynd ye not this purpose and entent, what is the qualitie[10] of the mooldes bytwene the nobles and you, nor the conveians[11] of the petygrie from Adam, nor the indifferens of your[12] soules in ther creacions. Be[13] not the prowder y[t] one price[14] redemyd both them and you, nor for y[t][15] that the glorie of all soules standith not in [bodely][16] power nor auctoritie, nor yet in syluer, gold nor precious stones, nor yet in bewtie, strengith, wisdome, nor yet in[17] pollicy, But only in vertue, indifferent to all creatures. But let [f. 74 d] vs all consyder y[t] god hath sett an[18] order by grace bytwene hym self and Angell,[19] and betwene Angell and Angell; and by reason betwene the[20] Angell and man, and betwene man

---

[1] C, H: "the widowes and the...".
[2] C, H: "that they".
[3] C, H: "and grudge".   [4] C.
[5] C, H: "muse theron nor disdaine ye not...".
[6] C, H: "our".   [7] Omitted in C, H.
[8] C, H.   [9] C, H: "do so".
[10] C, H: "or (H: nor) intent that is the equallitie".
[11] C, H: "cognisaunce".   [12] C, H: "their".
[13] C, H: "Nor be".   [14] C: "prince".
[15] Omitted in C, H.   [16] C, H. In A: "bloody".
[17] C, H omit "yet in".   [18] C, H: "a dew".
[19] C, H: "aungells".   [20] Omitted in C, H.

and man,[1] man and beest; And by nature only betwene beest and beest; which order, from the highest pointe to the lowest, god willyth vs fyrmely[2] to kepe withowt any enterprise to the contrary. Butt of all theis messages[3] y[t] theis proude[4] messengers brought vnto you, yf ye well[5] and substancially imprincte them in [the] hartes [of] the nobles [it should do][6] no harme; peraduenture yt wold cawse them at seasons to haue the more compassion, marcy and charitie on[7] the poore commyners.

And to put you in a more parfytt rememberance not to dele with this core[8] of lewde enterprise, Loke how your selfes and others[9] haue ben seruid and deceivid by hym in tymes past. First, consyder the greate enmytie[10] of the realme of France, being in greate wealth and tranquilitie. Loke on y[t] lewd[11] enterprise in the tyme of king   .[12] And at y[t] season frowardly did[13] thei greate and shamefull displeasures and wilfulnes to the nobles[14] of France. But in conclusion thei[15] were subdewid and vtterly distroid, And then was[16] the commons of Fraunce put in more subiection and thraldome then euer they were before, the which yet contynuyth. Loke more nere vnto your selfes, the comynaltie of this realme of England, who often tymes[17] smartyd righte[18] sore for such lewd entreprise.[19] Behold [well whether][20] ye commyners [f. 75] of the west parte of this land wan any honest[ie][21] or profytt by there lewde enterprise with ther capten the Black Smithe? I pray god save[22]

---

[1] C, H insert "and".

[2] C: "fervently": H omits the adverb.

[3] C, H: "messengers".   [4] C, H add "and sedicious".

[5] C, H: "will well".

[6] C, H. A runs: "in your hartes the nobles wold do you no...".

[7] C, H: "ouer".   [8] C, H: "lewd core".

[9] C, H: "and such as".   [10] Blank space in C, H.

[11] C, H: "Loke on them a lewde".

[12] Space of 2 inches in A.   [13] Omitted in C, H.

[14] C, H: "in the noblest".   [15] C: "there".

[16] C, H: "were".   [17] C: "haue oftentymes": H: "often".

[18] C, H: "full".   [19] H: "enterprises".

[20] C, H. In A: "what".   [21] C, H.   [22] C, H: "to saue".

this realme from any suche captein herafter. Therfor of thies presydentes ye haue enoughe to eschew this perillous core of your fruite; yet cast not away this enterprise of your core for it[1] may fortune to be to you a cheif frind. Therfore[2] kepe hym close within you vnto the tyme ye may lawfully vse hym.

Thus haue I[3] don with theis iiij[er] perillous cores of the[4] iiijer fruites. Now let this necessarie sawce be spoken of y[t] will serue well with all theis fower fruites, withowt the which sawce thies fower fruites ought not to be vsyd thoughe thei[5] be well paryd, as is before rehersyd. This

The drede
of god[6] sauce is nothing els but the dreede of god. Albeit this sawce be a lytle poynant[7] at the furst, yt is so holsom of yt[8] self y[t] it digestyth all maner of meates y[t] yt is vsyd [with],[9] and yt is a sawce righte agreable and convenyent for euery maner of[10] mete y[t] a christen man shold[11] eate. This sawce is[12] seruid to the poore and to the riche, to the syck and to the whole, and to all maner of people y[t] do vse[13] any of theis iiij[er] fruites.

Our souuereigne lord, when he vsyth his fruite[14] of honorable dignitie, he may not lack this[15] sawce, and it must be seruid to hym in the best maner.[16] And though this fruite of yt self[17] were ether tomotche dylicous and[18] had any other qualitie enfectyve, this poynant[19] sawce will take them all clerly away. And now this fruite of honorable dignitie when it is paryd,[20] y[t] is to say when the paringes of compassion [f. 75d] ar largly parid therfrom and bountuously

---

[1] H: "y[t]".
[2] C, H: "and therfore".   [3] C, H: "And thus I haue".
[4] C, H: "theis".   [5] C, H: "all they".
[6] H, C: "ye sawce".   [7] C, H: "pained".
[8] C, H use the masculine pronoun for "sauce".
[9] C, H.   [10] Omitted in C.
[11] C, H: "shall".   [12] Omitted in C, H.
[13] C, H: "that vseth".   [14] H: "useth fruites".
[15] C, H: "the".
[16] C, H: "be served (H: used) to him in the better".
[17] C, H: "fruite as of himself".   [18] C, H: "or".
[19] C leaves a blank space: omitted in H.   [20] C, H: "well pared".

distributyd where nede requerith, and the core therof,[1] which is elacion, not tochid but vsid with this souvereigne sawce of the dreede of god, It is a fruite parfytt and convenient for a christen king or a prince to vse.

And ye of the[2] devowt clergie in likewise, albeit your fruite of good example be[3] of it self mervilous good, and y[t] ye righte well and plentuously from yt do pare the paringes of the increase of vertue and connyng, and[4] righte discretly refuse subtyll glorie, the core therof, yet in any wise Vse all your good deedes and examples with[5] this profytable sawce, the drede of god, And the drede of his secrete iudgementes.[6] And then is your fruite of good example the very true examplerie and mirror of Christen [priestes].[7]

Also[8] ye of the noble Chyvalrie haue greate nede to vse this sawce of the drede of god abondantly with your[9] fruite of worldly prosperite, for, though ye[10] pare ther from the paringes[11] of trew defence righte diligently, and righte sewerly abstein[12] your selfes from the delectacion therof, his core, [it] is yet to you mutche[13] perillous to vse withowt the drede of god, This proper sawce. But so vsyd with fere yt is to the fruite righte mete and conuenyent for christen knightes.

And ye good commyners of this realme of England forbere ye not this sawce of y[e] fere[14] of god in vsyng of your fruite of tranquilite. For, though ye right busyly pare from your fruite for the profytt of your childeren the paringes of tymely[15] exercise, and also refuse righte wisely the core, which is lewd enterprise, yet thys sawce must ye nedes [f. 76] vse therwith, and[16] so vsyd it is the profitable and welthie fruite y[t] is requisyt and expedient for you, being

---

[1] H: "wherof".   [2] Omitted in C, H.   [3] H: "fruite be good, be".
[4] Omitted in C, H.   [5] H: "which".
[6] H: "judgment".   [7] C, H. A: "princes".
[8] C, H: "And also".   [9] H: "which the": C: "with the".
[10] H: "they".   [11] H: "paring".
[12] H: "and staying".
[13] C, H: "yet it (H omits) is to much".
[14] C, H: "dreade".   [15] C, H: "true".   [16] C, H: "but".

commyners of a Christen realme and vnder the obediens of a¹ most Christen king.

Peradue[n]ture ye will know when this noble sawce comyth, that necessarily yt² seruith aswell [for]³ theis iiijᵉʳ seuerall fruites, being of iiijᵉʳ seuerall natures, as also⁴ for all maner of people, of what degree, age, condicion or nature thei be of. This same is a iois⁵ or a lavatorie and⁶ springith or issuyth owt of the principall roote and owt of the tree of comen welth, which principall roote is callyd the loue of god, and issuyth and springith euer more conueniently with [the]⁷ most noble fruite yᵗ was rehersyd, which is the honour of god. For it is impossyble whersoeuer this principall roote, the loue [of]⁸ god, is fast and suerly rootyd yᵗ⁹ there shall not only growe and increase in habundant maner the fruite of the honour of god, But therwith this licor or sawce of the drede of god shall also plentuously spring and issue owt.

Yet peraduenture some will vnderstond and know what shalbe don with theis iiijer perillous cores, of whome so-motch danger was spoken. And forasmotche as it was aduisyd to kepe them as a store and not to cast them awaie, and also for yᵗ it was said it mighte fortune them to serue for some good purpose, therfor¹⁰ it shalbe necessarie to re-sorte to the vsing of the fyfth¹¹ fruite, which is the honor of god, and is the most excellent fruite of all¹² this tree of comen-wealthe. Somewhat it is tochid of the noblenes of thys fruite and that it was a fruite mete for all persons, of¹⁴ the which neuer grew disease, corruption or surfett. It is also yᵗ fruite yᵗ nedith non¹⁵ other sawce but baryth all goodnes in hym self. It¹⁶ hath no suche dangerous [f. 76 d] or perillous cores

[to eate the core]¹³

as were spoken of in the other iiij^{er} fruites, for it is of y^t nature y^t it will suffer nothing y^t ill is, or may become,[1] within yt. But this[2] good and glorious nature will couet to alter thinges[3] y^t be perillous and evill, and will make them good and behovefull.

For the proofe therof Let our souereigne lord take[4] the core of [the][5] fruite of honorable dignitie, which to vse therin was perillous and· venemous, But lett hym vse yt with this noble fruite and[6] the more good the fruite will do hym. But this fruite will somewhat alter the name of the core: yf ye callid [it, in] the fruite of worldly dignitie, vnreasonable elacion, ye shall call [it] now, [in] the noble fruite of ye honor of god, vertuous elacion, and yet it ys all[7] but one thing in effect.

And you lordes and masters[8] of the Clergie may bring forth the core of your[9] fruite of good example, that is glorie, y^t therin was[10] so pestiferous and wickyd, and vse yt with this noble fruite and see what harme yt shall do you.[11] For a suertie, no harme but mutche good, for the more ye glorie in this fruite ye better ye do. But for a better knolledge here wyll I put a certen addicion, [for] wher, in[12] our other fruite yt mighte be truly callyd vayne glorie, in this most noble fruite yt may be callyd[13] parfytt glorie.

Wher is now vain delectacion, this perillous and dangerous core of the fruite of worldly prosperitie, being the fruite of the chyvalrie? Ye noble [men][14] now bring hym forth and vse hym with this glorious fruite of thonour of god, for

---

[1] C, H: "may be to come".   [2] C, H: "his".
[3] C, H: "will come to alter all thinges".
[4] C, H: insert "elacion".   [5] C, H.
[6] Omitted in C, H.
[7] C, H: "the name of this core: if he were called into the fruite of... he shalbe called into this noble fruite...very elacion, and yet all it is".
[8] Omitted in C, H.   [9] C: "the".
[10] C, H: "was therein".   [11] Omitted in C, H.
[12] Written "wherin" in A.
[13] C, H: "here I will adde thereto a certaine Addicion, wherefore in our other fruite he might truly be called vaine glory, This most noble fruite will call him".   [14] C, H.

herwith it[1] is nothing noysom [but][2] neuerthelesse yt[3] is
verie necessarie, for this is the verie[4] fruite y^t ye should eate
[f. 77] at your libertie. Vse y^t core withall,[5] And now shall
he serue you righte well. And the name of this core must be
somewhat[6] changyd by this noble fruite, And y^t shalbe
from vain delectacion to trew exaltacion; all[7] is one substans.

And where is this lewd enterprise, the perillous core of the
fruite of tranquilitie y^t ye of the comynaltie haue suerly
kept and not Vsyd with[8] your fruite? Now bring yt forth
and vse yt at your libertie with this fruite, For the more ye
enterprise and the more often[9] ye make tobtein y^{is} fruite of
the honour of god the better ye do, for yt [is][10] the fruite y^t
all Christen people should [seek for]. And[11] where enterprise atteynith to your fruite of tranquilite yt was callyd
lewd enterprise, and in this excellent fruite yt may be callyd
noble enterprise.

And for the reward of this ordering your selves, ye
commyners, in thusing of your wealthie[12] fruite of tranquylitie, Ye shall not only haue righte synguler preise of the
people of other realmes and owtward parties,[13] but also a
great reward of god after this transytorie lyef. What preise[14]
shall hit be vnto you when all owtward people and commyners of all[15] other parties shall report you to be [the][16]
most pollitique and discrete commyners[17] of all Christen
realmes, and most wisely preserue your fruite of tranquilite,
not only with trew labor and parfytt concord emongist your
selfes, but also with faithfull reuerens to god and dew
obediens to your prince and superiors. And y^{ei} shall wisshe

[1] C, H: "he".   [2] C, H.
[3] C, H: "he".   [4] Omitted in C.
[5] C, H: "should and at your libertie may vse that core with".
[6] C, H: "somewhat be".   [7] C, H: "and all".
[8] C, H: "it with".
[9] C, H: "For the more enterprise and the oftener".
[10] C, H.   [11] C, H: "seek for, for".   [12] H: "worthie".
[13] C, H use "partes" throughout this passage.
[14] C, H: "a price".   [15] Omitted in C, H.
[16] C, H: "reporte of you to be the…".   [17] C, H: "commons".

them selfes to be in suche [f. 77 d] wealthy condicion as you be, or els to be sufferid to enherite emongist you.

But how farr aboue this shalbe the reward y^t god shall[1] gyve you when he shall say vnto you: "Now come ye vnto me, ye christen comyners and chosen people, which alwaies indeuerid[2] your selfes in trew labour and lawfull occupacion, withowt subtiltie or periurie, and haue kept well your roote of concord, and haue[3] not vsyd your welthy[4] tranquilite, the fruite of comen wealth, contrary to my lawes and commaundymentes, but haue diligently parid tymely exercise, the[5] paring therof, for the relyef of your childeren and seruantes, and haue not attemptyd any lewd enterprise, the core therof, to my dishonour, or[6] contrary to my ordynance. And ye be the people y^t never vysd [your][7] f[r]uite of wealthie tranquylitie But with the[8] sawce of my Drede. Also ye haue vsyd your princypall fruite to my honor, and therin haue you sett your core of lewd enterprise. Now come and haue your finall reward. For your trew worldly labor and besynes ye shalhaue perpetuall pleasures[9] and ease; for your good vnytie ·and comfort emongist your selfes ye shalbe vnyformyd[10] with Aungelles; for y^t ye haue kept your dewtie of[11] obediens to your prince and superiors I shall make you princes and superiors to all men and princes vpon the[12] erth; For y^t ye haue sett your enterprise in my honor and nothing to the contrary, therfor I[13] myself will be your capten to enterprise for you the celestiall Citie, where ye shall suerly enioye the fruite of tranquilite perpetuall. And for y^t ye haue vsyd [f. 78] the sauce of my dreed I shall sett you where you shall from hensforth for euer ioyefully[14] honour me, and neuer more painfully to

---

[1] C, H: "will".
[2] C, H: "the which haue alwaies busyed".
[3] Omitted in H.   [4] C, H: "your roote of".
[5] C, H: "truly   the".   [6] H: "and".
[7] C, H.   [8] C, H: "their".
[9] C, H: "pleasure".   [10] C, H: "informed".
[11] C, H: "for".   [12] Omitted in C, H.
[13] C, H: "nowe I...".   [14] Blank space in C, H.

drede me, nor nothing els. For ye be the lyving stones which shall[1] reedifye my heavenly Herusalem, in stede and place of the Angels which fell with Lucyfer[2] to hell, and ther to dwell for euermore."

But what shall the great fame and souereigne reward be that ye[3] of the noblest of the chivalrie shall haue of god and man for the well vsing of your fruite of the worldly[4] prosperitie in this realme of england? Ye may be suer y[t] all noble knightes of your greate fame will say: "Thies be the very trew christen knightes of whome all we may lerne to do our dewties[5] in the defence of the faith of the churche of Christ, and in trew redynes to serue the prince, to[6] defend hym and his realme. Let vs folloo the steppes of them for the honour of the[7] churche and the suertie of our prince, The wealth of our commens and the prosperitie of our selfes."

But what shall the souereigne reward be y[t] ye shall haue of god, when he shall say vnto you: "Now come ye to me, my chosen knightes, and I shall set you on the righte hand of my father, ther as his christen[8] knightes y[t] euer haue lovid the roote of trothe, and for no[9] worldly cawse wold swarve[10] ther from. And, for y[t] ye louid so well trothe, I shall ioyne you to my self with the indissoluble not of permane[n]t Love, for I am very troth whom [ye][11] haue lovid. And for y[t] ye haue vsyd your fruite of worldly prosperite according to my lawes and commaundymentes, now shall ye haue and take the swetenes of my prosperitie celestiall y[t] my father hathe gyven vnto me, and is ordenyd for me, and you as Brothern, before the creacion[12] of the world. And for y[t] you haue paryd your paringes of defens as my verie knightes [f. 78 d]to defend me and my churche militant, and

---

[1] C, H: "the loving stones which reedifie".
[2] C, H end sentence here.   [3] C, H: "that if ye".
[4] H: "the fruite of worldly...".
[5] C, H: "duty".
[6] C, H: "their Prince and to".   [7] C, H: "our".
[8] C, H: "father as his faithfull and christen".
[9] C, H: "none".   [10] C, H: "square".
[11] C, H. In A: "I".   [12] C, H: "constitucion".

haue byn¹ alweis redie to defend your king and his realme
with dew obediens, and, ouer yᵗ, haue gladly defendid the
poore widowes,² Orphanes, and all other my poore people,
[from]³ wronges and oppressions, and haue not appleid
your defence to defend false quarelles,⁴ murderers, theves
and extorcioners, I shalbe your protector and defendour
from all dangers and perilles in like wise as I protectyd my
chosen knighte, David. And for yᵗ ye haue not vsyd your
core of the fruyte, which is vain delectacion, with your
fruite of worldly prosperitie, ye shall drink your fyll and so
mutche yᵗ ye will desier, no more, of delectable grace and
mercy. And for yᵗ ye haue vsyd my sawce of my drede
with your fruite of wor[ld]ly prosperitie I shall sett you in
suche prosperous tryumphe yᵗ all earthly knightes shall
worship you, and all the devilles in hell shall drede you.
And for yᵗ you haue set your core of delectacion in the fruite
of my honor I shall make you the honorable knightes of my
deytie, and will say vnto you: 'Come, victorious knightes⁵
of christe, For ye Be thei yᵗ haue wonne the victorie ayenst
your most [mightie]⁶ ennymies, the Devill, the world and
the Fleashe,⁷ and them haue vtterly vanquisshed for euer.
Now take ye the places and romes and⁸ victorie with theis
knightes, St. Dionys,⁹ St. Mawrice and his fellowes, wher
thies ennymies nor any¹⁰ other shall have poore in anywise
to assault you or tempt¹¹ you, But shall flie from your faces
as the dust¹² doth from the farvent wyndes.'''¹³
    And ye vertuous Clergie, mark ye well¹⁴ what lawde of
this world and reward of god ye shalhaue for your parte by
you¹⁵ to be don, [f. 79] as is Before rehersyd. All the Clergie
of Christendome shall lawde you and say: "Theis be thei

---

¹ C, H: "and to be".   ² C, H insert "and".
³ C, H.   ⁴ C, H insert "and".
⁵ C, H omit "of my deytie...victorious knightes".
⁶ C, H. A: "victorious".   ⁷ C, H: "fleshe and the world".
⁸ C, H: "of".   ⁹ C, H insert "and".
¹⁰ Blank space in C: omitted in H.   ¹¹ C, H: "attempt".
¹² C, H: "light".   ¹³ C, H: "winde".
¹⁴ H omits "mark ye well".   ¹⁵ C, H omits "by you".

y^t be^1 the verie clerkes of Christes churche, that comme^2
truly by ther promotions without price,^{3} seruice or praier,
and be thei y^{t4} will not except nor take any promotions
But suche as thei know them selfes righte able in vertue and
conning to serue and kepe, and y^t gladly will refuse his owne
promotion to promote a more able person. Theis be thei y^t
forget not to pray dilige[n]tly and devowtly for the prince,
the Chivalrie and the^5 conmynaltie of ther realme, by
whome thei haue ther lyvinges, and put not in oblyuion
ther dewtie for ther founders, patrones and benefactors. Let
all vs take our lyghte of ther lantornes to serue god well."

But what worthie reward shall you haue of god, when he
shall say vnto you: "Now come to me, my Blyssyd pristes,
[on]^6 whose heades my holy vnction was not lost. Ye haue
consecratyd my verie^7 bodie with unpollutyd soules, nothing
defylyd with fylthines of your fleasshe. Ye haue trodden
vpon the steppes of humylitie with the yokes of chastitie
fastenyd on^8 your neckes. You haue kept your roote of
peace full salfly in word, deede^9 and thought, And, ouer y^t,
ye haue devoutly paryd your paringes^{10} y^t other may do the
same. Ye haue vsyd your fruite of good example to the
vttermost pointe withowt any Bleamyshe of your core of
vain glorie, and y^t aswell for charitie to^{11} your neighebors as
for the welthe of your owne soules. Ye haue plentuously
distributyd the paring^{12} of thencrease of vertue and connyng
to the best of your poores vnto the vnyuersyties and all oyer
places where you saw^{13} nede, withowt promotion of childeren
being yong in vertue or^{14} connyng, And specially to suche
romes [f. 79 d] as to vertuous and discrete Clerkes belongith.^{15}
Ye haue tastyd deply of the sawce of my drede in all the

^{1} C, H: "are". ^{2} C, H: "cometh".
^{3} H: "any price". ^{4} C, H: "which".
^{5} Omitted in H. ^{6} C, H. A: "by".
^{7} Omitted in C, H. ^{8} C, H: "in".
^{9} C, H: "full fervently in deede, word".
^{10} C, H omit "your paringes". ^{11} C, H: "of".
^{12} C, H: "paringes". ^{13} C, H: "shall".
^{14} C, H: "and". ^{15} C, H: "belonge".

vsing of your fruite of good example, and haue suerly
fyxid your glorie only in the fruite of my honour. Therfor
I will make you my parfytt priest[es]¹ for euer after myn
owne order. And, where before tyme ye haue consecratyd
my verie bodie² as in a shadow, ye shall fullie vse yt now as yt
is, and I shall transform you from³ the clernes of your faith
to yᵉ most clere⁴ fruycion of the godhed, and constytute
you for euer fellooes to myn appostelles, whose stepps you
haue followid."

But the most Christen king and most naturall lord, what
prese, lawde, or renowne shalhe⁵ haue, aswell of all Christen
princes as of the⁶ subiectes, for hauing⁷ this tree of comen
wealth in his realme in this manour two waies rootyd, in
hym self and in⁸ his subiectes, and plentuously garnisshed
with ther⁹ rehersyd fruites. For wher ther was greate preise
to the commens for ordering of yᵉᵐ selfes¹⁰ so yᵗ thei be in
suche wealth and tranquylytie,¹¹ the flower of yᵗ preise must
nedes sound to you, our souuereigne¹² lord, for setting and
keping them in yᵗ good order. And where your chyvalrie
be in noble fame for so doing ther dewtie, thei being¹³ in
suche worldly prosperitie, How motche more shall [ye]
haue¹⁴ of fame, lawde and drede, of whose proper example,
as of the princypall, yt doth procede.¹⁵ And if your clergie
haue greate lawdes¹⁶ for¹⁷ setting and plantyng of suche
vertuous prelates and other in the Churche of Christe within
your realme,¹⁸ How superhabon[dan]tly, aboue all thies,

¹ C, H.
² C, H: "where ye by fortune haue consecrated my body".
³ C, H omit "you from".   ⁴ C, H: "clerest".
⁵ C, H: "lawde and renowne shall ye...".
⁶ H: "their".   ⁷ C, H: "the having of...".
⁸ Omitted in C, H.   ⁹ C, H: "the".
¹⁰ C, H omit "of". H: "him selfe".
¹¹ C, H: "in much welthy tranquillity".
¹² C, H: "to your soveraigne".
¹³ C, H: "that they be".   ¹⁴ A: "shalhaue".
¹⁵ C, H: "shall he (H: ye) have for whose lawde and dreade and by
whose example the principall doth it".
¹⁶ H: "laude".   ¹⁷ C, H: insert "the".   ¹⁸ C, H insert "but".

shall your preise,[1] lawde [f. 80] and renowne be for the vertuous and prudent ordering of your most royall person, and specially in your yeres of florisshing youthe, Wherby this noble tree of commenwealthe is thus honorably rootyd and florisshid with delycate fruite[2] within this realme, and like to the tree of a Christen king, for the which all other kinges and princes shall wisshe most hartely to be in Like case and condicion. And at the last, though for disdain and highe mynd thei will not speke yt, Yet, be ye suer, thei will well consyder yt, with greate fere and drede to displease you.

And aboue all this, what glorious reward shall ye haue of god, the king of all kinges, your maker and redemor, when he shall saie vnto you: "Now come to me, you[3] Christen king and knighte. Thou arte he y[t] haste rulyd my people according to my will and pleasure. Thou hast more delyted in my[4] loue, the principall roote of the tree of comenwealth of this realme, then thou hast in thine auctoritie, power and[5] pleasure. Thou hast knowne at all tymes to haue receivyd power, auctoritie and regaltie only of me. Thou hast ministrid to all my people, [thy][6] subiectes, trew iustice euer more, and wisely[7] foresene to whom thou hast commyttyd thy greate power and highe auctorite in that behalf, and hast not disorderid[8] iustice for any profytt, affection or cawse toching thei self. Thou hast not reisyd new lawes or customes for thy singuler profytt to the comen hurt of thy subiectes, but yf any suche before thy daies were reysyd,[9] or any good lawe subuertyd, thou hast by thy charitable mynd forborne thy subiectes, and redusyd all thinges to thold and good customes,[10] and so during thy lief hast kept yt. Thou hast not also lenyd to[11] synyster counsell of any person that wold induce

---

[1] C, H add "fame".
[2] C, H: "fruites".
[3] C, H: "my".
[4] C, H: "hast delighted more my".
[5] H: "or".
[6] C, H. A: "thies".
[7] C, H: "hast wiselie".
[8] C, H: "dishonoured".
[9] C: "araised".
[10] C, H add "and constitutions".
[11] C, H: "also beleved the".

the contrary, But rather hast ponysshed suche persons in example of other. Thou hast sett my churche in good [f. 80d] order in[1] promoting of vertuous and conyng men withowt any point of Symonie, and causyd them to kepe there dioces and cures withowt disturbance of fre election. Thou hast kept the[2] temporall subiectes in a loving drede, and hast not sufferyd them, nor the mightest of them, toppresse the poore, nor yet woldes not[3] suffer thyn owne seruantes to extort or wring[4] any other of my people, thy subiectes, nor hast not sufferid the nobles of thy realme, nor any other of thei subiectes [so] to rune at riot[5] as to ponisshe or reuenge there owne quarelles. Thou hast supportyd thy[6] comynaltie in a good tranquilitie, and hast not sufferid them to fall into Idlenes. Thou hast ben trew in thy deedes and promises, and, as nighe as thou mighte,[7] hast cawsyd all thy subiectes to be the same, and hast cawsyd thyne officers and seruantes to paie y^e[8] poore subiectes truly ther dewties. Thou hast kept them all, from the highest degre to the lowest, in a good concord and vnytie emongist them selves, and hast also kept them by thy greate studdie, wisdom and pollicie, in good peace, withowt warr.[9] And thou art y^t king which hast euer vsyd the fruite of honorable dignitie to my pleasure and contentacion, without any vnreasonable elacion aboue the[10] lowest parte of thy reason, and therwith hast thou vsyd the sawce of my drede with as meke a harte as the poorest subiect in[11] thy realm. And forthermore thou hast aboue all thinges iudgid in execution of my honour and to glorifie my name.

Wherfore come now to me and reigne with me as[12] my glorious knight and Christen king, my dere sonne, my good

---

[1] C, H: "as well in".   [2] C, H: "thy".
[3] Omitted in C, H.   [4] C, H: "wrong".
[5] Blank space in C, H for "run at riot".
[6] C, H: "the".   [7] C, H: "mightest".
[8] C, H: "thy officers...paie thy".
[9] C, H: "peace with owtward princes".
[10] C, H: "of the same above thy".
[11] C, H: "of".   [12] Omitted in C, H.

and[1] singuler belouid brother in manhode,[2] my verie felloo in creacion of thy soule. I shall annoynte the a king eternall with the holie oyle y[t] issuith[3] owt of the bosome of my father, and crowne the with the crowne of myn owne immortall glorie and honour. And now [f. 81] shall thy subiectes, thou also and I, be made as on thing, and shall alwaies be togethers glorified with the Clerenes of my father, and so reigne and contynew in the howse[4] of my father[5] for euer, wher shalbe contynuall light withowt darcknes, perpetuall peace withowt warr or debate, And all delectacion and swetines withowt any displeasure or grief, all rest and pleasure withowt labor or pain, all ioye and felicitie withowt any thoughte or[6] sorrow, and euer to lyve withowt disease or sicknes, and our desiers to be vtterly satisfied withowt studie or busynes. The sight of our father shalbe our[7] foode to kepe vs from hunger and[8] thurst; his mantell of loue shall so wrapp vs y[t] we shall neuer feele heete ne cold. And, [wheras] before thou were worshipid and seruid as a king with fraile and mortall people, thy regaltie[9] shall now be suche y[t] the Aungelles of heaven shall honour the as a king immortall, and mynister vnto the. And this tyme with the shall neuer passe nor waste, and so shall[10] thou for euer see me and honour me in thy selfe and thy self in me." To the which kingdom Christe Iesu, that bought vs all with his precious Blood, bring our said souereigne lord and his trew subiectes, togethers with all christen people. Amen.

[f. 81 d] Thus endith this symple and rude treatise callid the tree of comenwealth, mad by a person most ignorant and being also[11] in worldly vexacion and troblid with[12] the sorrofull and bytter rememberans of death. In the beginning

---

[1] C, H: "my godhead, my".
[2] C, H: "by the manhood".
[3] C, H: "Elie that issued".   [4] C: "honor".
[5] H omits "and so reigne...of my father".
[6] C, H: "touche of".   [7] C, H: "your".
[8] Repeated in H.   [9] C: "Regally".
[10] C, H: "shalt".   [11] Omitted in C, H.
[12] C, H: "and trowble, also with".

of which treatise[1] it is some what tochid of the trew rememberance of god, which furst[2] aboue all thinges is to be
don, aswell with kinges and princes as[3] with all other; and
most specially with the greate kinges and princes, who haue
greate cawse[4] for y[t][5] thei haue most of his guyftes. And
then a word or two haue ben[6] spoken of certen necessarie[7]
and behovefull properties or condicions in a king or a[8]
prince to be had for his honour and suertie.

Then,[9] folling, yt hath ben shewid of this tree of comenwealth. The which tree most nedes haue fyve rootes to bare
hym suerly vprighte, as hath ben rehersyd: y[t] is to say, the
furst and principall roote, the loue of god, which in any
wise may not be forborn from[10] this tree of comon wealth
in a Christen realme. Thother iiij[er] rootes[11] be iustice, trothe,
concord and peax. And, corespondent to theis fyve rootes,
this tree shall plentuously bare [five][12] noble fruites. The most
excellent and cheif fruite is the honour of god, which springith
owt of the roote of the tree, the trew loue[13] of god, withowt
the which all thother be but lytle wourth in a Christen
realme. Thother iiij[er] fruites be theis: the fruite of honorable
dignitie only appropriatyd to the king and to his disposicion,
which growith by the reason of the roote of Iustice: The
second is the fruite of good example righte necessarie for
the Clergie, and y[t] issuith owt of the roote of peace: The
third is worldly prosperitie [f. 82] ordenyd principally for
the chivalrie, which springith owt of the roote of trothe:
The fowerth and last[14] of thies iiij[er] fruites is the fruite of
profytable tranquilitie necessarie[15] for the commynaltie, and
growith owt of the roote of concord.

---

[1] C, H: "beginning wherof".   [2] C, H insert "and".
[3] C, H: "and".
[4] C, H: "for they haue greatest cause".
[5] Repeated in C.   [6] Omitted in H.
[7] C, H: "necessaries".   [8] Omitted in C.
[9] C, H: "and then".   [10] C, H: "to".
[11] C, H: "and the fowre rootes".   [12] "Fower" in all texts.
[13] C, H: "roote of the true Love".
[14] C, H: "the laste".   [15] C, H: "full necessarie".

It is also rememberid y^t theis iiij^{er} last fruites haue iiij^{er} seuerall paringes righte behovefull to be paryd and distri- butyd vnto them y^t haue nede yerof. First, the paring of the fruite of honorable dignitie is compassion or pyttie. The paring of the fruite of good example is thencrease of vertue and conning. The paring of the fruite of worldly prosperitie is trew defens. The paring of the fruite of profytable tran- quylitie is tymely exercise. It also hath ben[1] consyderid that theis iiij^{er} last fruites haue iiij^{er} dyuerse perillous cores which in any wise may not be vsyd with theis fruites but be[2] re- seruid for some other purpose. The perillous core of the fruite of honorable dignitie is vnreasonable elacion. The pestiferous[3] core of the fruite of good example is subtyll glorie or glorificacion. The dangerous core of the fruite of worldly prosperitie is vain delectacion. And the noysom core of the fruite of profytable tranquilitie is lewd enter- prise.

It hath also ben somewhat shewid how theis iiijer last fruites must be vsyd by discrecion, and how euery parte shall nedes[4] be vsyd with the sawce of the drede of god, [f. 82 d] and how this[5] same kind of sawce will serue for all theis iiijer fruites, Also[6] how y^t sawce is a lycor or ioyesse[7] y^t issuith owt of the principall roote, which is the loue of god. It hath be[ne][8] mocioned y^t all theis iiij^{er} perillous cores rehersyd will right well agre with the furst fruite, which is the honour of god. And y^t the same furst fruite is so worthie and so noble of his nature y^t he will suffer no perillous core, nor any[9] other evill thing, to be within hym, But will rather converte all evill to good. This is the fruite of the[10] which all princes and oyer, noble men[11] and vnnoble, the riche and the poore, the yong and the olde, the sick and

---

[1] C, H: "hath bene also".   [2] C, H: "to be".
[3] C, H: "pestilenciall".
[4] C, H: "shalbe contented with his owne proper fruite, And when and howe all theis fowre fruites muste needes".   [5] C, H: "the".
[6] C, H: "and".   [7] C: "a Jewce".
[8] C, H.   [9] C, H: "noe".
[10] Omitted in C, H.   [11] H: "man".

the whole, may vse yt[1] at ther libertie withowt danger, controling or delyuerance. Last[2], and fynallie, it hath ben declarid what reward, aswell worldly as hevenly, our souereigne lord and euery one of his subiectes, that is to say, euery person in his degre, shalhaue for doing ther dewties to kepe vp this tree[3] of comenwealth within this realme of England, in maner and forme before rehersyd[4] and declarid.

[1] Omitted in C.
[2] C, H: "or disturbance. And last".
[3] C, H: "noble tree".
[4] C, H end at "aboue rehearsed".

FINIS

INDEX

Alderkirk (Lincolnshire), 13

Belknap, Edward, "master of the prerogative", 4–5

Bishops, 16, 32, 33, 42

Bramshott, Elizabeth, 1, 8

Bramshott, John, 1, 8

Bramshott, William, 8

Bramshott (Hampshire), 1, 8

Bray, Sir Reginald, 3, 10 n.

Bromley, William, 13–14

Calbourne (Isle of Wight), 1, 8

"Capten the Black Smithe" [1497], 91

Chancery, Inns of, 2; record of titles in, 8

Charles the Great, 30

Chivalry, 44–5, 48, 54, 56, 57, 58, 59, 66–7, 68, 77, 86, 89, 90, 93, 95, 98–9, 100, 101, 105

Church, 16, 21, 22, 24–6, 43, 45, 62, 64, 66, 98, 100, 101, 103

Clergy, 15, 24–6, 42–4, 48, 56–7, 58, 59, 62–6, 71, 77, 89, 93, 95, 99–101, 105

Commissioners, enquiry into concealments, 7, 8; special and general, 34, 35

Commonalty (commoners, commons), 15, 45–8, 55, 56, 57, 58, 59, 67, 87–92, 93–4, 96–8, 100, 101, 103, 105

Commons, House of, Speaker of, 3; "the comen house", 9 n.

D'Ewes, Sir Simonds, 12

Dread of God, the sauce, 60, 92–4, 97, 99, 100–101, 103, 106

Dudley, Andrew, 1 n.

Dudley, Edmund, autobiographical references, 21–3, 104; career, 1–11; political ideas, 14–16

Dudley, Elizabeth, 1 n.

Dudley, Jerome, 1 n., 16 n.

Dudley, John of Atherington (Sussex), 1, 3

Dudley, John, Duke of Northumberland, 1 n., 13

Dudley, John, Lord Dudley (de Sutton), 1, 3

Dudley, Peter, 1

Dudley, Robert, Earl of Leicester, 12

Dudley, William, Bishop of Durham, 1

Education, of children, 14, 45, 67–8, 97; at universities, 14, 26, 62–6, 100

Edward the Confessor, "St", 30

Edward IV, 29

Empson, Sir Richard, Chancellor of the Duchy of Lancaster, 3, 5, 8, 9

England, 11, 22, 23, 25, 26, 33, 45, 48, 49, 91, 93, 98, 107

Ernley, John, Attorney-General, 3, 7

Fitz William, Sir William, 6

Frowyk, Thomas, 4, 15 n.

Fruits of the "Tree", 51–3, 60, 94, 95, 101–2, 105, 106; see also Good Example, Honorable Dignity, Honour of God, Tranquillity, Worldly Prosperity

Gatcombe (Isle of Wight), 1, 8

Good Example, the fruit of, 51, 52, 56, 57, 58, 71, 93, 95, 100–1, 105, 106; Increase of Virtue and Cunning, the paring of, 62–6; Subtle, or vain, glory, the core of, 71–7, 95

Gray's Inn, 2

Grey, Elizabeth and John, Viscount Lisle, 1 n.

Harold, 28–9

Henry III, 29

Henry VII, 3, 4, 6, 7, 8, 10, 13, 15, 16, 21, 22; character of, 29; will of, 24

For EU product safety concerns, contact us at Calle de José Abascal, 56–1°,
28003 Madrid, Spain or eugpsr@cambridge.org.

www.ingramcontent.com/pod-product-compliance
Ingram Content Group UK Ltd.
Pitfield, Milton Keynes, MK11 3LW, UK
UKHW012337130625
459647UK00009B/349